YOUR
HO

2019

LIBRA

YOUR PERSONAL HOROSCOPE 2019

LIBRA

24th September–23rd October

igloobooks

igloobooks

Published in 2018
by Igloo Books Ltd
Cottage Farm
Sywell
NN6 0BJ
www.igloobooks.com

FIR003 0718
2 4 6 8 10 9 7 5 3 1
ISBN: 978-1-78810-536-1

This is an abridged version of material originally published
in Old Moore's Horoscope and Astral Diary.

Cover designed by Nicholas Gage
Edited by Bobby Newlyn-Jones

Printed and manufactured in China

CONTENTS

INTRODUCTION

Your personal horoscopes have been specifically created to allow you to get the most from astrological patterns and the way they have a bearing on not only your zodiac sign, but nuances within it. Using the diary section of the book you can read about the influences and possibilities of each and every day of the year. It will be possible for you to see when you are likely to be cheerful and happy or those times when your nature is in retreat and you will be more circumspect. The diary will help to give you a feel for the specific 'cycles' of astrology and the way they can subtly change your day-to-day life. For example, when you see the sign ☿, this means that the planet Mercury is retrograde at that time. Retrograde means it appears to be running backwards through the zodiac. Such a happening has a significant effect on communication skills, but this is only one small aspect of how the personal horoscope can help you.

With your personal horoscope the story doesn't end with the diary pages. It includes simple ways for you to work out the zodiac sign the Moon occupied at the time of your birth, and what this means for your personality. In addition, if you know the time of day you were born, it is possible to discover your Ascendant, yet another important guide to your personal make-up and potential.

Many readers are interested in relationships and in knowing how well they get on with people of other astrological signs. You might also be interested in the way you appear to very different sorts of individuals. If you are such a person, the section on Venus will be of particular interest. Despite the rapidly changing position of this planet, you can work out your Venus sign, and learn what bearing it will have on your life.

Using your personal horoscope you can travel on one of the most fascinating and rewarding journeys that anyone can take – the journey to a better realisation of self.

THE ESSENCE OF LIBRA

Exploring the Personality of Libra the Scales

(24TH SEPTEMBER – 23RD OCTOBER)

What's in a sign?

At heart you may be the least complicated of all the zodiac sign types, though your ruling element is Air, and that is always going to supply some surprises. Diplomatic, kind and affectionate, your nature blows like a refreshing breeze through the lives of almost anyone you meet. It isn't like you to be gloomy for very long at a time, and you know how to influence the world around you.

It's true that you don't like dirt, or too much disorganisation, and you tend to be very artistic by inclination. You get your own way in life, not by dint of making yourself unpopular in any way but rather with the sort of gentle persuasion to which almost everyone you know falls victim at one time or another. Being considerate of others is more or less second nature to you, though you may not be quite as self-sacrificing as sometimes appears to be the case. You definitely know what you want from life and are not above using a little subterfuge when it comes to getting it.

You are capable and resourceful, but just a little timid on occasions. All the same, when dealing with subject matter that you know and relish, few can better you out there in the practical world. You know how to order your life and can be just as successful in a career sense as you tend to be in your home life. There are times when personal attractions can be something of a stumbling block because you love readily and are very influenced by the kindness and compliments of those around you.

Librans do need to plan ahead, but don't worry about this fact too much because you are also extremely good at thinking on your feet. Getting others to do your bidding is a piece of cake because you are not tardy when it comes to showing your affections. Nevertheless you need to be careful not to allow yourself to fall into unreliable company, or to get involved in schemes that seem too good to be true – some of them are. But for most of the time you present a happy picture to the world and get along just fine, with your ready smile and adaptable personality. You leave almost any situation happier and more contented than it was when you arrived.

Libra resources

When it comes to getting on in life you have as much ammunition in your armoury as most zodiac signs and a great deal more than some. For starters you are adaptable and very resourceful. When you have to take a leap in logic there is nothing preventing you from doing so, and the strong intuition of which your zodiac sign is capable can prove to be very useful at times.

One of your strongest points is the way you manage to make others love you. Although you might consider yourself to be distinctly 'ordinary', that's not the way the world at large perceives you. Most Librans have the ability to etch themselves onto the minds of practically everyone they come across. Why? It's simple. You listen to what people have to say and appear to be deeply interested. On most occasions you are, but even if the tale is a tedious one you give the impression of being rooted to the spot with a determination to hear the story right through. When it comes to responding you are extremely diplomatic and always manage to steer a sensible course between any two or more opposing factions.

Having said that you don't like dirt or untidy places, this is another fact that you can turn to your advantage, because you can always find someone who will help you out. So charming can Libra be that those who do all they can to make you more comfortable regularly end up feeling that you have done them a favour.

It is the sheer magic of the understated Libran that does the trick every time. Even on those rare occasions when you go out with all guns blazing to get what you want from life, you are very unlikely to make enemies on the way. Of course you do have to be careful on occasions, like everyone, but you can certainly push issues further than most. Why? Mainly because people don't realise that you are doing so.

You could easily sell any commodity – though it might be necessary to believe in it yourself first. Since you can always see the good points in anything and tend to be generally optimistic, that should not be too problematical either.

Beneath the surface

In many respects Libra could be the least complicated sign of the zodiac so it might be assumed that 'what you see is what you get'. Life is rarely quite that simple, though you are one of the most straightforward people when it comes to inner struggle. The fact is that most Librans simply don't have a great deal. Between subconscious motivation and in-your-face action there is a seamless process. Librans do need to be loved and this fact can be quite a strong motivation in itself towards any particular course of action. However, even this desire for affection isn't the most powerful factor when considering the sign of the Scales.

What matters most to you is balance, which is probably not at all surprising considering what your zodiac sign actually means. Because of this you would go to tremendous lengths to make sure that your inner resolves create the right external signs and actions to offer the peace that you are looking for most of all.

Like most people born under the Air signs you are not quite as confident as you sometimes appear to be. In the main you are modest and not given to boasting, so you don't attract quite the level of attention of your fellow Air signs, Gemini and Aquarius. All the same you are quite capable of putting on an act when it's necessary to give a good account of yourself in public. You could be quaking inside but you do have the ability to hide this from the world at large.

Librans exhibit such a strong desire to be kind to everyone they meet that they may hide their inner feelings from some people altogether. It's important to remember to be basically honest, even if that means upsetting others a little. This is the most difficult trait for Libra to deal with and may go part of the way to explaining why so many relationship break-ups occur for people born under this zodiac sign. However, as long as you find ways and means to explain your deepest emotional needs, at least to those you love, all should be well.

In most respects you tend to be an open book, particularly to those who take the trouble to look. Your nature is not over-deep, and you are almost certainly not on some secret search to find the 'real you'. Although Libra is sometimes accused of being superficial there are many people in the world who would prefer simplicity to complications and duplicity.

Making the best of yourself

This may be the easiest category by far for the zodiac sign of Libra. The fact is that you rarely do anything else but offer the best version of what you are. Presentation is second nature to Libra, which just loves to be noticed. Despite this you are naturally modest and so not inclined to go over the top in company. You can be relied upon to say and do the right things for most of the time. Even when you consider your actions to be zany and perhaps less acceptable, this is not going to be the impression that the majority of people would get.

In a work sense you need to be involved in some sort of occupation that is clean, allows for a sense of order and ultimately offers the ability to use your head as well as your hands. The fact is that you don't care too much for unsavoury sorts of work and need to be in an environment that suits your basically refined nature. If the circumstances are right you can give a great deal to your work and will go far. Librans also need to be involved with others because they are natural co-operators. For this reason you may not be at your best when working alone or in situations that necessitate all the responsibilities being exclusively yours.

When in the social mainstream you tend to make the best of yourself by simply being what you naturally are. You don't need frills and fancies. Libra is able to make the best sort of impression by using the natural qualities inherent in the sign. As a result, your natural poise, your ability to cut through social divisions, your intelligence and your adaptability should all ensure that you remain popular.

What may occasionally prove difficult is being quite as dominant as the world assumes you ought to be. Many people equate efficiency with power. This is not the way of people born under the Scales, and you need to make that fact plain to anyone who seems to have the desire to shape you.

The impressions you give

Although the adage 'what you see is what you get' may be truer for Libra than for any of its companion signs, it can't be exclusively the case. However, under almost all circumstances you are likely to make friends. You are a much shrewder operator than sometimes appears to be the case and tend to weigh things in the balance very carefully. Libra can be most things to most people, and that's the sort of adaptability that ensures success at both a social and a professional level.

The chances are that you are already well respected and deeply liked by most of the people you know. This isn't so surprising since you are not inclined to make waves of any sort. Whether or not this leads to you achieving the degree of overall success that you deserve in life is quite a different matter. When impressions count you don't tend to let yourself down, or the people who rely on you. Adapting yourself to suit different circumstances is the meat and drink of your basic nature and you have plenty of poise and charm to disarm even the most awkward of people.

In affairs of the heart you are equally adept at putting others at their ease. There is very little difficulty involved in getting people to show their affection for you and when it comes to romance you are one of the most successful practitioners to be found anywhere. The only slight problem in this area of life, as with others, is that you are so talented at offering people what they want that you might not always be living the sort of life that genuinely suits you. Maybe giving the right impression is a little too important for Libra. A deeper form of honesty from the start would prevent you from having to show a less charming side to your nature in the end.

In most circumstances you can be relied upon to exhibit a warm, affectionate, kind, sincere and interesting face to the world at large. As long as this underpins truthfulness it's hard to understand how Libra could really go far wrong.

The way forward

You must already be fairly confident that you have the necessary skills and natural abilities to get on well in a world that is also filled with other people. From infancy most Librans learn how to rub along with others, whilst offering every indication that they are both adaptable and amenable to change. Your chameleon-like ability to 'change colour' in order to suit prevailing circumstances means that you occasionally drop back to being part of the wallpaper in the estimation of at least some people. A greater ability to make an impression probably would not go amiss sometimes, but making a big fuss isn't your way and you actively seek an uncomplicated sort of life.

Balance is everything to Libra, a fact that means there are times when you end up with nothing at all. What needs to be remembered is that there are occasions when everyone simply has to make a decision. This is the hardest thing in the world for you to do but when you manage it you become even more noticed by the world at large.

There's no doubt that people generally hold you in great affection. They know you to be quite capable and love your easy-going attitude to life. You are rarely judgmental and tend to offer almost anyone the benefit of the doubt. Although you are chatty, and inclined to listen avidly to gossip, it isn't your natural way to be unkind, caustic or backbiting. As a result it would seem that you have all the prerequisites to live an extremely happy life. Alas, things are rarely quite that easy.

It is very important for you to demonstrate to yourself, as well as to others, that you are an individual with thoughts and feelings of your own. So often do you defer to the needs of those around you that the real you gets somewhat squashed on the way. There have to be times when you are willing to say 'yes' or 'no' unequivocally, instead of a noncommittal 'I don't really mind' or 'whatever you think best'. At the end of the day you do have opinions and can lead yourself into the path of some severe frustrations if you are unwilling to voice them in the first place.

Try to be particularly honest in deep, emotional attachments. Many Libran relationships come to grief simply because there isn't enough earthy honesty present in the first place. People knowing how you feel won't make them care for you any less. A fully integrated, truthful Libran, with a willingness to participate in the decision making, turns out to be the person who is both successful and happy.

14

LIBRA ON THE CUSP

Astrological profiles are altered for those people born at either the beginning or the end of a zodiac sign, or, more properly, on the cusps of a sign. In the case of Libra this would be on the 24th of September and for two or three days after, and similarly at the end of the sign, probably from the 21st to the 23rd of October.

The Virgo Cusp – 24th September to 26th September

Here we find a Libran subject with a greater than average sense of responsibility and probably a better potential for success than is usually the case for Libra when taken alone. The Virgoan tendency to take itself rather too seriously is far less likely when the sign is mixed with Libra and the resultant nature is often deeply inspiring, and yet quite centred. The Virgo-cusp Libran has what it takes to break through the red tape of society, and yet can understand the need for its existence in the first place. You are caring and concerned, quick on the uptake and very ready to listen to any point of view but, at the end of the day, you know when it is going to be necessary to take a personal stance and this you are far more willing to do than would be the case for non-cuspid Librans.

Family members are important to you, but you always allow them their own individuality and won't get in the way of their personal need to spread their own wings, even at times when it's hard to take this positive stance. Practically speaking, you are a good home-maker but you also enjoy travelling and can benefit greatly from seeing the way other cultures think and behave. It is true that you can have the single-mindedness of a Virgoan, but even this aspect is modified by the Libran within you, so that you usually try to see alternative points of view and often succeed in doing so.

At work you really come into your own. Not only are you capable enough to deal with just about any eventuality, you are also willing to be flexible and to make up your mind instantly when it proves necessary to do so. Colleagues and subordinates alike tend to trust you. You may consider self-employment, unlike most Librans who are usually very worried by this prospect. Making your way in life is something you tend to take for granted, even when the going gets tough.

What people most like about you is that, despite your tremendously practical approach to life, you can be very zany and retain a sense of fun that is, at its best, second to none. Few people find you difficult to understand or to get on with in a day-to-day sense.

The Scorpio Cusp – 21st October to 23rd October

The main difference between this cusp and the one at the Virgo end of Libra, is that you tend to be more emotionally motivated and of a slightly less practical nature. Routines are easy for you to address, though you can become very restless and tend to find your own emotional responses difficult to deal with. Sometimes even you don't understand what makes you tick, and that can be a problem. Actually you are not as complicated as you may have come to believe. It's simply that you have a unique view of life and one that doesn't always match that of the people around you, but as Libra instinctively wants to conform, this can lead to some personal confusion.

In family matters you are responsible, very caring and deeply committed to others. It's probable that you work in some field that finds you in direct contact with the public at large and many Scorpio-cusp Librans choose welfare, social or hospital work as a first choice. When it comes to love, you are flexible in your choice and the necessary attributes to promote a long-lasting and happy relationship are clearly present in your basic nature. If there are problems, they may come about as a result of your inability to choose properly in the first place, because you are the first to offer anyone the benefit of the doubt.

When it comes to the practicalities of life, Scorpio can prove to be extremely useful. It offers an 'edge' to your nature and, as Scorpio is a Fixed sign, you are less likely to lose ground because of lack of confidence than Libra alone would be. Your future can be bright, but only if you are willing to get involved in something that really interests you in the first place. You certainly do not care for getting your hands dirty and tend to gravitate towards more refined positions.

Creative potential is good and you could be very artistic, though if this extends to fine art, at least some of your pictures will have 'dark' overtones that might shock some people, including yourself. At base you are kind, caring, complicated, yet inspiring.

LIBRA AND ITS ASCENDANTS

The nature of every individual on the planet is composed of the rich variety of zodiac signs and planetary positions that were present at the time of their birth. Your Sun sign, which in your case is Libra, is one of the many factors when it comes to assessing the unique person you are. Probably the most important consideration, other than your Sun sign, is to establish the zodiac sign that was rising over the eastern horizon at the time that you were born. This is your Ascending or Rising sign. Most popular astrology fails to take account of the Ascendant, and yet its importance remains with you from the very moment of your birth, through every day of your life. The Ascendant is evident in the way you approach the world, and so, when meeting a person for the first time, it is this astrological influence that you are most likely to notice first. Our Ascending sign essentially represents what we appear to be, while the Sun sign is what we feel inside ourselves.

The Ascendant also has the potential for modifying our overall nature. For example, if you were born at a time of day when Libra was passing over the eastern horizon (this would be around the time of dawn) then you would be classed as a double Libran. As such, you would typify this zodiac sign, both internally and in your dealings with others. However, if your Ascendant sign turned out to be a Water sign, such as Pisces, there would be a profound alteration of nature, away from the expected qualities of Libra.

One of the reasons why popular astrology often ignores the Ascendant is that it has always been rather difficult to establish. We have found a way to make this possible by devising an easy-to-use table, which you will find on page 157 of this book. Using this, you can establish your Ascendant sign at a glance. You will need to know your rough time of birth, then it is simply a case of following the instructions.

For those readers who have no idea of their time of birth it might be worth allowing a good friend, or perhaps your partner, to read through the section that follows this introduction. Someone who deals with you on a regular basis may easily discover your Ascending sign, even though you could have some difficulty establishing it for yourself. A good understanding of this component of your nature is essential if you want to be aware of that 'other person' who is responsible for the way you make contact with the world at large. Your Sun sign, Ascendant sign, and the other pointers in this book will, together, allow you a far better understanding of what makes you tick as an individual. Peeling back the different layers of your astrological make-up can be an enlightening experience, and the Ascendant may represent one of the most important layers of all.

Libra with Libra Ascendant

There is no doubt that you carry the very best of all Libran worlds in your nature, though at the same time there is a definite possibility that you often fall between two stools. The literal advice as a result is that you must sometimes make a decision, even though it isn't all that easy for you to do so. Not everyone understands your easy-going side and there are occasions when you could appear to be too flippant for your own good.

The way you approach the world makes you popular, and there is no doubt at all that you are the most diplomatic person to be found anywhere in the length and breadth of the zodiac. It is your job in life to stop people disagreeing and since you can always see every point of view, you make a good impression on the way.

Relationships can sometimes be awkward for you because you can change your mind so easily. But love is never lacking and you can be fairly certain of a generally happy life. Over-indulging is always a potential problem for Air-sign people such as yourself, and there are times in your life when you must get the rest and relaxation which is so important in funding a strong nervous system. Drink plenty of water to flush out a system that can be over-high in natural salts.

Libra with Scorpio Ascendant

There is some tendency for you to be far more deep than the average Libran would appear to be, and for this reason it is crucial that you lighten up from time to time. Every person with a Scorpio quality needs to remember that there is a happy and carefree side to all events, and your Libran quality should allow you to bear this in mind. Sometimes you try to do too many things at the same time. This is fine if you take the casual overview of Libra, but less sensible when you insist on picking the last bone out of every potential, as is much more the case for Scorpio.

When worries come along, as they sometimes will, be able to listen to what your friends have to say and also realise that they are more than willing to work on your behalf, if only because you are so loyal to them. You do have a quality of self-deception, but this should not get in the way too much if you combine the instinctive actions of Libra with the deep intuition of your Scorpio component.

Probably the most important factor of this combination is your ability to succeed in a financial sense. You make a good manager, but not of the authoritarian sort. Jobs in the media or where you are expected to make up your mind quickly would suit you because there is always an underpinning of practical sense that rarely lets you down.

Libra with Sagittarius Ascendant

A very happy combination this, with a great desire for life in all its forms and a need to push forward the bounds of the possible in a way that few other zodiac sign connections would do. You don't like the unpleasant or ugly in life and yet you are capable of dealing with both if you have to. Giving so much to humanity, you still manage to retain a degree of individuality that would surprise many, charm others, and please all.

On the reverse side of the same coin you might find that you are sometimes accused of being fickle, but this is only an expression of your need for change and variety, which is endemic to both these signs. True, you have more of a temper than would be the case for Libra when taken on its own, but such incidents would see you up and down in a flash, and it is almost impossible for you to bear a grudge of any sort. Routines get on your nerves and you are far happier when you can please yourself and get ahead at your own pace, which is quite fast.

As a lover you can make a big impression and most of you will not go short of affection in the early days, before you choose to commit yourself. Once you do, there is always a chance of romantic problems, but these are less likely when you have chosen carefully in the first place.

Libra with Capricorn Ascendant

It is a fact that Libra is the most patient of the Air signs, though like the others it needs to get things done fairly quickly. Capricorn, on the other hand, will work long and hard to achieve its objectives and will not be thwarted in the end. As a result this is a quite powerful sign combination and one that should lead to ultimate success.

Capricorn is often accused of taking itself too seriously and yet it has an ironic and really very funny sense of humour which only its chief confidants recognise. Libra is lighthearted, always willing to have fun and quite anxious to please. When these two basic types come together in their best forms, you might find yourself to be one of the most well-balanced people around. Certainly you know what you want, but you don't have to use a bulldozer in order to get it.

Active and enthusiastic when something really takes your fancy, you might also turn out to be one of the very best lovers of them all. The reason for this is that you have the depth of Capricorn but the lighter and more directly affectionate qualities of the Scales. What you want from life in a personal sense, you eventually tend to get, but you don't care too much if this takes you a while. Few people could deny that you are a faithful friend, a happy sort and a deeply magnetic personality.

Libra with Aquarius Ascendant

Stand by for a truly interesting and very inspiring combination here, but one that is sometimes rather difficult to fathom, even for the sort of people who believe themselves to be very perceptive. The reason for this could be that any situation has to be essentially fixed and constant in order to get a handle on it, and this is certainly not the case for the Aquarian–Libran type. The fact is that both these signs are Air signs, and to a certain extent as unpredictable as the wind itself.

To most people you seem to be original, frank, free and very outspoken. Not everything you do makes sense to others, and if you were alive during the hippy era, it is likely that you went around with flowers in your hair, for you are a free-thinking idealist at heart. With age you mature somewhat, but never too much, because you will always see the strange, the comical and the original in life. This is what keeps you young and is one of the factors that makes you so very attractive to members of the opposite sex. Many people will want to 'adopt' you, and you are at your very best when in company.

Much of your effort is expounded on others and yet, unless you discipline yourself a good deal, personal relationships of the romantic sort can bring certain difficulties. Careful planning is necessary.

Libra with Pisces Ascendant

An Air and Water combination, you are not easy to understand and have depths that show at times, surprising those people who thought they already knew what you were. You will always keep people guessing and are just as likely to hitchhike around Europe as you are to hold down a steady job, both of which you would undertake with the same degree of commitment and success. Usually young at heart, but always carrying the potential for an old head on young shoulders, you are something of a paradox and not at all easy for totally 'straight' types to understand. But you always make an impression and tend to be very attractive to members of the opposite sex.

In matters of health you do have to be a little careful because you dissipate much nervous energy and can sometimes be inclined to push yourself too hard, at least in a mental sense. Frequent periods of rest and meditation will do you the world of good and should improve your level of wisdom, which tends to be fairly high already. Much of your effort in life is expounded on behalf of humanity as a whole, for you care deeply, love totally and always give of your best. Whatever your faults and failings might be, you are one of the most popular people around.

Libra with Aries Ascendant

Libra has the tendency to bring out the best in any zodiac sign, and this is no exception when it comes together with Aries. You may, in fact, be the most comfortable of all Aries types, simply because Libra tempers some of your more assertive qualities and gives you the chance to balance out opposing forces, both inside yourself and in the world outside. You are fun to be with and make the staunchest friend possible. Although you are generally affable, few people would try to put one over on you because they would quickly come to know how far you are willing to go before you let forth a string of invective that would shock those who previously underestimated your basic Aries traits.

Home and family are very dear to you, but you are more tolerant than some Aries types are inclined to be and you have a youthful zest for life that should stay with you no matter what age you manage to achieve. There is always something interesting to do and your mind is a constant stream of possibilities. This makes you very creative and you may also demonstrate a desire to look good at all times. You may not always be quite as confident as you appear to be, but few would guess the fact.

Libra with Taurus Ascendant

A fortunate combination in many ways, this is a double-Venus rulership, since both Taurus and Libra are heavily reliant on the planet of love. You are social, amiable and a natural diplomat, anxious to please and ready to care for just about anyone who shows interest in you. You hate disorder, which means that there is a place for everything and everything in its place. This can throw up the odd paradox however, since being half Libran you cannot always work out where that place ought to be! You deal with life in a humorous way and are quite capable of seeing the absurd in yourself, as well as in others. Your heart is no bigger than that of the quite typical Taurean, but it sits rather closer to the surface and so others recognise it more.

On those occasions when you know you are standing on firm ground you can show great confidence, even if you have to be ready to change some of your opinions at the drop of a hat. When this happens you can be quite at odds with yourself, because Taurus doesn't take very many U-turns, whereas Libra does. Don't expect to know yourself too well, and keep looking for the funny side of things, because it is within humour that you forge the sort of life that suits you best.

Libra with Gemini Ascendant

What a happy-go-lucky soul you are and how popular you tend to be with those around you. Libra is, like Gemini, an Air sign and this means that you are the communicator par excellence, even by Gemini standards. It can sometimes be difficult for you to make up your mind about things because Libra does not exactly aid this process, and especially not when it is allied to Mercurial Gemini. Frequent periods of deep thought are necessary, and meditation would do you a great deal of good. All the same, although you might sometimes be rather unsure of yourself, you are rarely without a certain balance. Clean and tidy surroundings suit you the best, though this is far from easy to achieve because you are invariably dashing off to some place or other, so you really need someone to sort things out in your absence.

The most important fact of all is that you are much loved by your friends, of which there are likely to be very many. Because you are so willing to help them out, in return they are usually there when it matters and they would probably go to almost any length on your behalf. You exhibit a fine sense of justice and will usually back those in trouble. Charities tend to be attractive to you and you do much on behalf of those who live on the fringes of society or people who are truly alone.

Libra with Cancer Ascendant

What an absolutely pleasant and approachable sort of person you are, and how much you have to offer. Like most people associated with the sign of Cancer you give yourself freely to the world, and will always be on hand if anyone is in trouble or needs the special touch you can bring to almost any problem. Behaving in this way is the biggest part of what you are and so people come to rely on you very heavily. Like Libra you can see both sides of any coin and you exhibit the Libran tendency to jump about from one foot to the other when it is necessary to make decisions relating to your own life. This is not usually the case when you are dealing with others however, because the cooler and more detached qualities of Cancer will show through in these circumstances.

It would be fair to say that you do not deal with routines as well as Cancer alone might do and you need a degree of variety in your life, which in your case often comes in the form of travel, which can be distant and of long duration. It isn't unusual for people who have this zodiac combination to end up living abroad, though even this does little to prevent you from getting itchy feet from time to time. In romance you show an original quality that keeps the relationship young and working very well.

Libra with Leo Ascendant

Libra brings slightly more flexibility to the fixed quality of the Leo nature. On the whole you do not represent a picture that is so much different from other versions of the Lion, though you find more time to smile, enjoy changing your mind a great deal more and have a greater number of casual friends. Few would find you proud or haughty and you retain the common touch that can be so important when it comes to getting on in life generally. At work you like to do something that brings variety, and would probably soon tire of doing the same task over and over again. Many of you are teachers, for you have patience, allied to a stubborn core. This can be an indispensable combination on occasions and is part of the reason for the material success that many folk with this combination of signs achieve.

It isn't often that you get down in the dumps, after all there is generally something more important around the next corner, and you love the cut and thrust of everyday life. You always manage to stay young at heart, no matter what your age might be, and you revel in the company of interesting and stimulating types. Maybe you should try harder to concentrate on one thing at once and also strive to retain a serious opinion for more than ten minutes at a time. However, Leo helps to control your flighty tendencies.

Libra with Virgo Ascendant

Libra has the ability to lighten almost any load, and it is particularly good at doing so when it is brought together with the much more repressed sign of Virgo. To the world at large you seem relaxed, happy and able to cope with most of the pressures that life places upon you. Not only do you deal with your own life in a bright and breezy manner but you are usually on hand to help others out of any dilemma that they might make for themselves. With excellent powers of communication, you leave the world at large in no doubt whatsoever concerning both your opinions and your wishes. It is in the talking stakes that you really excel because Virgo brings the silver tongue of Mercury and Libra adds the Air-sign desire to be in constant touch with the world outside your door.

You like to have a good time and can often be found in the company of interesting and stimulating people, who have the ability to bring out the very best in your bright and sparkling personality. Underneath however, there is still much of the worrying Virgoan to be found and this means that you have to learn to relax inside as well as appearing to do so externally. In fact you are much more complex than most people would realise, and definitely would not be suited to a life that allowed you too much time to think about yourself.

THE MOON AND THE PART IT PLAYS IN YOUR LIFE

In astrology the Moon is probably the single most important heavenly body after the Sun. Its unique position, as partner to the Earth on its journey around the solar system, means that the Moon appears to pass through the signs of the zodiac extremely quickly. The zodiac position of the Moon at the time of your birth plays a great part in personal character and is especially significant in the build-up of your emotional nature.

Your Own Moon Sign

Discovering the position of the Moon at the time of your birth has always been notoriously difficult because tracking the complex zodiac positions of the Moon is not easy. This process has been reduced to three simple stages with our Lunar Tables. A breakdown of the Moon's zodiac positions can be found from page 35 onwards, so that once you know what your Moon Sign is, you can see what part this plays in the overall build-up of your personal character.

If you follow the instructions on the next page you will soon be able to work out exactly what zodiac sign the Moon occupied on the day that you were born and you can then go on to compare the reading for this position with those of your Sun sign and your Ascendant. It is partly the comparison between these three important positions that goes towards making you the unique individual you are.

How To Discover Your Moon Sign

This is a three-stage process. You may need a pen and a piece of paper but if you follow the instructions below the process should only take a minute or so.

STAGE 1 First of all you need to know the Moon Age at the time of your birth. If you look at Moon Table 1, on page 33, you will find all the years between 1921 and 2019 down the left side. Find the year of your birth and then trace across to the right to the month of your birth. Where the two intersect you will find a number. This is the date of the New Moon in the month that you were born. You now need to count forward the number of days between the New Moon and your own birthday. For example, if the New Moon in the month of your birth was shown as being the 6th and you were born on the 20th, your Moon Age Day would be 14. If the New Moon in the month of your birth came after your birthday, you need to count forward from the New Moon in the previous month. Whatever the result, jot this number down so that you do not forget it.

STAGE 2 Take a look at Moon Table 2 on page 34. Down the left hand column look for the date of your birth. Now trace across to the month of your birth. Where the two meet you will find a letter. Copy this letter down alongside your Moon Age Day.

STAGE 3 Moon Table 3 on page 34 will supply you with the zodiac sign the Moon occupied on the day of your birth. Look for your Moon Age Day down the left hand column and then for the letter you found in Stage 2. Where the two converge you will find a zodiac sign and this is the sign occupied by the Moon on the day that you were born.

Your Zodiac Moon Sign Explained

You will find a profile of all zodiac Moon Signs on pages 35 to 38, showing in yet another way how astrology helps to make you into the individual that you are. In each daily entry of the Astral Diary you can find the zodiac position of the Moon for every day of the year. This also allows you to discover your lunar birthdays. Since the Moon passes through all the signs of the zodiac in about a month, you can expect something like twelve lunar birthdays each year. At these times you are likely to be emotionally steady and able to make the sort of decisions that have real, lasting value.

MOON TABLE 1

YEAR	AUG	SEP	OCT	YEAR	AUG	SEP	OCT	YEAR	AUG	SEP	OCT
1921	3	2	1/30	1954	28	27	26	1987	24	23	22
1922	22	21	20	1955	17	16	15	1988	12	11	10
1923	12	10	10	1956	6	4	4	1989	1/31	29	29
1924	30	28	28	1957	25	23	23	1990	20	19	18
1925	19	18	17	1958	15	13	12	1991	9	8	8
1926	8	7	6	1959	4	3	2/31	1992	28	26	25
1927	27	25	25	1960	22	21	20	1993	17	16	15
1928	16	14	14	1961	11	10	9	1994	7	5	5
1929	5	3	2	1962	30	28	28	1995	26	24	24
1930	24	22	20	1963	19	17	17	1996	14	13	11
1931	13	12	11	1964	7	6	5	1997	3	2	2/31
1932	2/31	30	29	1965	26	25	24	1998	22	20	20
1933	21	19	19	1966	16	14	14	1999	11	10	8
1934	10	9	8	1967	5	4	3	2000	29	27	27
1935	29	27	27	1968	24	23	22	2001	19	17	17
1936	17	15	15	1969	12	11	10	2002	8	6	6
1937	6	4	4	1970	2	1	1/30	2003	27	26	25
1938	25	23	23	1971	20	19	19	2004	14	13	12
1939	15	13	12	1972	9	8	8	2005	4	3	2
1940	4	2	1/30	1973	28	27	26	2006	23	22	21
1941	22	21	20	1974	17	16	15	2007	13	12	11
1942	12	10	10	1975	7	5	5	2008	1/31	30	29
1943	1/30	29	29	1976	25	23	23	2009	20	19	18
1944	18	17	17	1977	14	13	12	2010	10	8	8
1945	8	6	6	1978	4	2	2/31	2011	29	27	27
1946	26	25	24	1979	22	21	20	2012	17	16	15
1947	16	14	14	1980	11	10	9	2013	6	4	4
1948	5	3	2	1981	29	28	27	2014	24	23	22
1949	24	23	21	1982	19	17	17	2015	15	13	12
1950	13	12	11	1983	8	7	6	2016	2	1	30
1951	2	1	1/30	1984	26	25	24	2017	22	20	20
1952	20	19	18	1985	16	14	14	2018	11	9	9
1953	9	8	8	1986	5	4	3	2019	30	28	27

TABLE 2   MOON TABLE 3

DAY	SEP	OCT	M/D	X	Y	Z	a	b	d	e
1	X	a	0	VI	VI	LI	LI	LI	LI	SC
2	X	a	1	VI	LI	LI	LI	LI	SC	SC
3	X	a	2	LI	LI	LI	LI	SC	SC	SC
4	Y	b	3	LI	LI	SC	SC	SC	SC	SA
5	Y	b	4	LI	SC	SC	SC	SA	SA	SA
6	Y	b	5	SC	SC	SC	SA	SA	SA	CP
7	Y	b	6	SC	SA	SA	SA	CP	CP	CP
8	Y	b	7	SA	SA	SA	SA	CP	CP	AQ
9	Y	b	8	SA	SA	CP	CP	CP	CP	AQ
10	Y	b	9	SA	CP	CP	CP	AQ	AQ	AQ
11	Y	b	10	CP	CP	CP	AQ	AQ	AQ	PI
12	Y	b	11	CP	AQ	AQ	AQ	PI	PI	PI
13	Y	b	12	AQ	AQ	AQ	PI	PI	PI	AR
14	Z	d	13	AQ	AQ	PI	PI	AR	PI	AR
15	Z	d	14	PI	PI	PI	AR	AR	AR	TA
16	Z	d	15	PI	PI	PI	AR	AR	AR	TA
17	Z	d	16	PI	AR	AR	AR	AR	TA	TA
18	Z	d	17	AR	AR	AR	AR	TA	TA	GE
19	Z	d	18	AR	AR	AR	TA	TA	GE	GE
20	Z	d	19	AR	TA	TA	TA	TA	GE	GE
21	Z	d	20	TA	TA	TA	GE	GE	GE	CA
22	Z	d	21	TA	GE	GE	GE	GE	CA	CA
23	Z	d	22	GE	GE	GE	GE	CA	CA	CA
24	a	e	23	GE	GE	GE	CA	CA	CA	LE
25	a	e	24	GE	CA	CA	CA	CA	LE	LE
26	a	e	25	CA	CA	CA	CA	LE	LE	LE
27	a	e	26	CA	LE	LE	LE	LE	VI	VI
28	a	e	27	LE	LE	LE	LE	VI	VI	VI
29	a	e	28	LE	LE	LE	VI	VI	VI	LI
30	a	e	29	LE	VI	VI	VI	VI	LI	LI
31	–	e								

AR = Aries, TA = Taurus, GE = Gemini, CA = Cancer, LE = Leo, VI = Virgo,
LI = Libra, SC = Scorpio, SA = Sagittarius, CP = Capricorn, AQ = Aquarius, PI = Pisces

MOON SIGNS

Moon in Aries

You have a strong imagination, courage, determination and a desire to do things in your own way and forge your own path through life.

Originality is a key attribute; you are seldom stuck for ideas although your mind is changeable and you could take the time to focus on individual tasks. Often quick-tempered, you take orders from few people and live life at a fast pace. Avoid health problems by taking regular time out for rest and relaxation.

Emotionally, it is important that you talk to those you are closest to and work out your true feelings. Once you discover that people are there to help, there is less necessity for you to do everything yourself.

Moon in Taurus

The Moon in Taurus gives you a courteous and friendly manner, which means you are likely to have many friends.

The good things in life mean a lot to you, as Taurus is an Earth sign that delights in experiences which please the senses. Hence you are probably a lover of good food and drink, which may in turn mean you need to keep an eye on the bathroom scales, especially as looking good is also important to you.

Emotionally you are fairly stable and you stick by your own standards. Taureans do not respond well to change. Intuition also plays an important part in your life.

Moon in Gemini

You have a warm-hearted character, sympathetic and eager to help others. At times reserved, you can also be articulate and chatty: this is part of the paradox of Gemini, which always brings duplicity to the nature. You are interested in current affairs, have a good intellect, and are good company and likely to have many friends. Most of your friends have a high opinion of you and would be ready to defend you should the need arise. However, this is usually unnecessary, as you are quite capable of defending yourself in any verbal confrontation.

Travel is important to your inquisitive mind and you find intellectual stimulus in mixing with people from different cultures. You also gain much from reading, writing and the arts but you do need plenty of rest and relaxation in order to avoid fatigue.

Moon in Cancer

The Moon in Cancer at the time of birth is a fortunate position as Cancer is the Moon's natural home. This means that the qualities of compassion and understanding given by the Moon are especially enhanced in your nature, and you are friendly and sociable and cope well with emotional pressures. You cherish home and family life, and happily do the domestic tasks. Your surroundings are important to you and you hate squalor and filth. You are likely to have a love of music and poetry.

Your basic character, although at times changeable like the Moon itself, depends on symmetry. You aim to make your surroundings comfortable and harmonious, for yourself and those close to you.

Moon in Leo

The best qualities of the Moon and Leo come together to make you warm-hearted, fair, ambitious and self-confident. With good organisational abilities, you invariably rise to a position of responsibility in your chosen career. This is fortunate as you don't enjoy being an 'also-ran' and would rather be an important part of a small organisation than a menial in a large one.

You should be lucky in love, and happy, provided you put in the effort to make a comfortable home for yourself and those close to you. It is likely that you will have a love of pleasure, sport, music and literature. Life brings you many rewards, most of them as a direct result of your own efforts, although you may be luckier than average and ready to make the best of any situation.

Moon in Virgo

You are endowed with good mental abilities and a keen receptive memory, but you are never ostentatious or pretentious. Naturally quite reserved, you still have many friends, especially of the opposite sex. Marital relationships must be discussed carefully and worked at so that they remain harmonious, as personal attachments can be a problem if you do not give them your full attention.

Talented and persevering, you possess artistic qualities and are a good homemaker. Earning your honours through genuine merit, you work long and hard towards your objectives but show little pride in your achievements. Many short journeys will be undertaken in your life.

Moon in Libra

With the Moon in Libra you are naturally popular and make friends easily. People like you, probably more than you realise, you bring fun to a party and are a natural diplomat. For all its good points, Libra is not the most stable of astrological signs and, as a result, your emotions can be a little unstable too. Therefore, although the Moon in Libra is said to be good for love and marriage, your Sun sign and Rising sign will have an important effect on your emotional and loving qualities.

You must remember to relate to others in your decision-making. Co-operation is crucial because Libra represents the 'balance' of life that can only be achieved through harmonious relationships. Conformity is not easy for you because Libra, an Air sign, likes its independence.

Moon in Scorpio

Some people might call you pushy. In fact, all you really want to do is to live life to the full and protect yourself and your family from the pressures of life. Take care to avoid giving the impression of being sarcastic or impulsive and use your energies wisely and constructively.

You have great courage and you invariably achieve your goals by force of personality and sheer effort. You are fond of mystery and are good at predicting the outcome of situations and events. Travel experiences can be beneficial to you.

You may experience problems if you do not take time to examine your motives in a relationship, and also if you allow jealousy, always a feature of Scorpio, to cloud your judgement.

Moon in Sagittarius

The Moon in Sagittarius helps to make you a generous individual with humanitarian qualities and a kind heart. Restlessness may be intrinsic as your mind is seldom still. Perhaps because of this, you have a need for change that could lead you to several major moves during your adult life. You are not afraid to stand your ground when you know your judgement is right, you speak directly and have good intuition.

At work you are quick, efficient and versatile and so you make an ideal employee. You need work to be intellectually demanding and do not enjoy tedious routines.

In relationships, you anger quickly if faced with stupidity or deception, though you are just as quick to forgive and forget. Emotionally, there are times when your heart rules your head.

Moon in Capricorn

The Moon in Capricorn makes you popular and likely to come into the public eye in some way. The watery Moon is not entirely comfortable in the Earth sign of Capricorn and this may lead to some difficulties in the early years of life. An initial lack of creative ability and indecision must be overcome before the true qualities of patience and perseverance inherent in Capricorn can show through.

You have good administrative ability and are a capable worker, and if you are careful you can accumulate wealth. But you must be cautious and take professional advice in partnerships, as you are open to deception. You may be interested in social or welfare work, which suit your organisational skills and sympathy for others.

Moon in Aquarius

The Moon in Aquarius makes you an active and agreeable person with a friendly, easy-going nature. Sympathetic to the needs of others, you flourish in a laid-back atmosphere. You are broad-minded, fair and open to suggestion, although sometimes you have an unconventional quality which others can find hard to understand.

You are interested in the strange and curious, and in old articles and places. You enjoy trips to these places and gain much from them. Political, scientific and educational work interests you and you might choose a career in science or technology.

Money-wise, you make gains through innovation and concentration and Lunar Aquarians often tackle more than one job at a time. In love you are kind and honest.

Moon in Pisces

You have a kind, sympathetic nature, somewhat retiring at times, but you always take account of others' feelings and help when you can.

Personal relationships may be problematic, but as life goes on you can learn from your experiences and develop a better understanding of yourself and the world around you.

You have a fondness for travel, appreciate beauty and harmony and hate disorder and strife. You may be fond of literature and would make a good writer or speaker yourself. You have a creative imagination and may come across as an incurable romantic. You have strong intuition, maybe bordering on a mediumistic quality, which sets you apart from the mass. You may not be rich in cash terms, but your personal gifts are worth more than gold.

LIBRA IN LOVE

Discover how compatible you are with people from the same and other signs of the zodiac. Five stars equals a match made in heaven!

Libra meets Libra

This is a potentially successful match because Librans are extremely likeable people, and so it stands to reason that two Librans together will be twice as pleasant and twice as much fun. However, Librans can also be indecisive and need an anchor from which to find practical and financial success, and obviously one Libran won't provide this for another. Librans can be flighty in a romantic sense, so both parties will need to develop a steadfast approach for a long-term relationship. Star rating: ****

Libra meets Scorpio

Many astrologers have reservations about this match because, on the surface, the signs are so different. However, this couple may find fulfilment because these differences mean that their respective needs are met. Scorpio needs a partner to lighten the load which won't daunt Libra, while Libra looks for a steadfast quality which it doesn't possess, but Scorpio can supply naturally. Financial success is possible because they both have good ideas and back them up with hard work and determination. All in all, a promising outlook. Star rating: ****

Libra meets Sagittarius

Libra and Sagittarius are both adaptable signs who get on well with most people, but this promising outlook often does not follow through because each brings out the flighty side of the other. This combination is great for a fling, but when the romance is over someone needs to see to the practical side of life. Both signs are well meaning, pleasant and kind, but are either of them constant enough to build a life together? In at least some of the cases, the answer would be no. Star rating: ***

Libra meets Capricorn

Libra and Capricorn rub each other up the wrong way because their attitudes to life are so different, and although both are capable of doing something about this, in reality they probably won't. Capricorn is steady, determined and solid, while Libra is bright but sometimes superficial and not entirely reliable. They usually lack the instant spark needed to get them together in the first place, so when it does happen it is often because one of the partners is not typical of their sign. Star rating: **

Libra meets Aquarius

One of the best combinations imaginable, partly because both are Air signs and so share a common meeting point. But perhaps the more crucial factor is that both signs respect each other. Aquarius loves life and originality, and is quite intellectual. Libra is similar, but more balanced and rather less eccentric. A visit to this couple's house would be entertaining and full of zany wit, activity and excitement. Both are keen to travel and may prefer to 'find themselves' before taking on too many domestic responsibilities. Star rating: *****

Libra meets Pisces

Libra and Pisces can be extremely fond of each other, even deeply in love, but this alone isn't a stable foundation for long-term success. Pisces is extremely deep and doesn't even know itself very well. Libra may initially find this intriguing but will eventually feel frustrated at being unable to understand the Piscean's emotional and personal feelings. Pisces can be jealous and may find Libra's flightiness difficult, which Libra can't stand. They are great friends and they may make it to the romantic stakes, but when they get there a lot of effort will be necessary. Star rating: ***

Libra meets Aries

These are zodiac opposites which means a make-or-break situation. The match will either be a great success or a dismal failure. Why? Well, Aries finds it difficult to understand the flighty Air-sign tendencies of Libra, whilst the natural balance of Libra contradicts the unorthodox Arian methods. Any flexibility will come from Libra, which may mean that things work out for a while, but Libra only has so much patience and it may eventually run out. In the end, Aries may be just too bossy for an independent but sensitive sign like Libra. Star rating: **

Libra meets Taurus

A happy life is important to both these signs and, as they are both ruled by Venus, they share a common understanding, even though they display themselves so differently. Taurus is quieter than Libra, but can be decisive, and that's what counts. Libra is interested in absolutely everything, an infectious quality when seen through Taurean eyes. The slightly flighty qualities of Libra may lead to jealousy from the Bull. Not an argumentative relationship and one that often works well. There could be many changes of address for this pair. Star rating: ****

Libra meets Gemini

One of the best possible zodiac combinations. Libra and Gemini are both Air signs, which leads to a meeting of minds. Both signs simply love to have a good time, although Libra is the tidiest and less forgetful. Gemini's capricious nature won't bother Libra, who acts as a stabilising influence. Life should generally run smoothly, and any rows are likely to be short and sharp. Both parties genuinely like each other, which is of paramount importance in a relationship and, ultimately, there isn't a better reason for being or staying together. Star rating: *****

Libra meets Cancer

Almost anyone can get on with Libra, which is one of the most adaptable signs of them all. But being adaptable does not always lead to fulfilment and a successful match here will require a quiet Libran and a slightly more progressive Cancerian than the norm. Both signs are pleasant and polite, and like domestic order, but Libra may find Cancer too emotional and perhaps lacking in vibrancy, while Libra, on the other hand, may be a little too flighty for steady Cancer. Star rating: ***

Libra meets Leo

The biggest drawback here is likely to be in the issue of commitment. Leo knows everything about constancy and faithfulness, a lesson which, sadly, Libra needs to learn. Librans are easy-going and diplomatic, qualities which are useful when Leo is on the war-path. This couple should be compatible on a personal level and any problems tend to relate to the different way in which these signs deal with outside factors. With good will and an open mind, it can work out well enough. Star rating: ***

Libra meets Virgo

There have been some rare occasions when this match has found great success, but usually the darker and more inward-looking Virgoan depresses the naturally gregarious Libran. Libra appears self-confident, but is not so beneath the surface, and needs encouragement to develop inner confidence, which may not come from Virgo. Constancy can be a problem for Libra, who also tires easily and may find Virgo dull. A lighter, less serious approach to life from Virgo is needed to make this work. Star rating: **

VENUS:
THE PLANET OF LOVE

If you look up at the sky around sunset or sunrise you will often see Venus in close attendance to the Sun. It is arguably one of the most beautiful sights of all and there is little wonder that historically it became associated with the goddess of love. But although Venus does play an important part in the way you view love and in the way others see you romantically, this is only one of the spheres of influence that it enjoys in your overall character.

Venus has a part to play in the more cultured side of your life and has much to do with your appreciation of art, literature, music and general creativity. Even the way you look is responsive to the part of the zodiac that Venus occupied at the start of your life, though this fact is also down to your Sun sign and Ascending sign. If, at the time you were born, Venus occupied one of the more gregarious zodiac signs, you will be more likely to wear your heart on your sleeve, as well as to be more attracted to entertainment, social gatherings and good company. If on the other hand Venus occupied a quiet zodiac sign at the time of your birth, you would tend to be more retiring and less willing to shine in public situations.

It's good to know what part the planet Venus plays in your life for it can have a great bearing on the way you appear to the rest of the world and since we all have to mix with others, you can learn to make the very best of what Venus has to offer you.

One of the great complications in the past has always been trying to establish exactly what zodiac position Venus enjoyed when you were born because the planet is notoriously difficult to track. However, we have solved that problem by creating a table that is exclusive to your Sun sign, which you will find on the following page.

Establishing your Venus sign could not be easier. Just look up the year of your birth on the next page and you will see a sign of the zodiac. This was the sign that Venus occupied in the period covered by your sign in that year. If Venus occupied more than one sign during the period, this is indicated by the date on which the sign changed, and the name of the new sign. For instance, if you were born in 1950, Venus was in Virgo until the 4th October, after which time it was in Libra. If you were born before 4th October your Venus sign is Virgo, if you were born on or after 4th October, your Venus sign is Libra. Once you have established the position of Venus at the time of your birth, you can then look in the pages which follow to see how this has a bearing on your life as a whole.

1921 LEO / 26.9 VIRGO /
    21.10 LIBRA
1922 SCORPIO / 11.10 SAGITTARIUS
1923 LIBRA / 16.10 SCORPIO
1924 LEO / 8.10 VIRGO
1925 SCORPIO / 12.10 SAGITTARIUS
1926 VIRGO / 6.10 LIBRA
1927 VIRGO
1928 LIBRA / 29.9 SCORPIO
1929 LEO / 26.9 VIRGO /
    20.10 LIBRA
1930 SCORPIO / 12.10 SAGITTARIUS
1931 LIBRA / 15.10 SCORPIO
1932 LEO / 7.10 VIRGO
1933 SCORPIO / 11.10 SAGITTARIUS
1934 VIRGO / 5.10 LIBRA
1935 VIRGO
1936 LIBRA / 28.9 SCORPIO
1937 LEO / 25.9 VIRGO /
    20.10 LIBRA
1938 SCORPIO / 14.10 SAGITTARIUS
1939 LIBRA / 14.10 SCORPIO
1940 LEO / 7.10 VIRGO
1941 SCORPIO / 11.10 SAGITTARIUS
1942 VIRGO / 5.10 LIBRA
1943 VIRGO
1944 LIBRA / 28.9 SCORPIO
1945 LEO / 25.9 VIRGO /
    19.10 LIBRA
1946 SCORPIO / 14.10 SAGITTARIUS
1947 LIBRA / 13.10 SCORPIO
1948 LEO / 7.10 VIRGO
1949 SCORPIO / 11.10 SAGITTARIUS
1950 VIRGO / 4.10 LIBRA
1951 VIRGO
1952 LIBRA / 27.9 SCORPIO
1953 VIRGO / 19.10 LIBRA
1954 SCORPIO / 16.10 SAGITTARIUS
1955 LIBRA / 12.10 SCORPIO
1956 LEO / 6.10 VIRGO
1957 SCORPIO / 10.10 SAGITTARIUS
1958 VIRGO / 4.10 LIBRA
1959 VIRGO / 28.9 LEO
1960 LIBRA / 27.9 SCORPIO
1961 VIRGO / 18.10 LIBRA
1962 SCORPIO / 16.10 SAGITTARIUS
1963 LIBRA / 12.10 SCORPIO
1964 LEO / 6.10 VIRGO
1965 SCORPIO / 9.10 SAGITTARIUS
1966 VIRGO / 4.10 LIBRA
1967 VIRGO / 3.10 LIBRA
1968 LIBRA / 26.9 SCORPIO
1969 VIRGO / 17.10 LIBRA
1970 SCORPIO / 19.10 SAGITTARIUS

1971 LIBRA / 11.10 SCORPIO
1972 LEO / 6.10 VIRGO
1973 SCORPIO / 9.10 SAGITTARIUS
1974 VIRGO / 3.10 LIBRA
1975 VIRGO / 5.10 LEO
1976 LIBRA / 26.9 SCORPIO
1977 VIRGO / 17.10 LIBRA
1978 SCORPIO / 19.10 SAGITTARIUS
1979 LIBRA / 11.10 SCORPIO
1980 LEO / 5.10 VIRGO
1981 SCORPIO / 9.10 SAGITTARIUS
1982 VIRGO / 3.10 LIBRA
1983 VIRGO / 7.10 LEO
1984 LIBRA / 25.9 SCORPIO
1985 VIRGO / 16.10 LIBRA
1986 SCORPIO
1987 LIBRA / 10.10 SCORPIO
1988 LEO / 5.10 VIRGO
1989 SCORPIO / 8.10 SAGITTARIUS
1990 VIRGO / 2.10 LIBRA
1991 VIRGO / 8.10 LEO
1992 LIBRA / 25.9 SCORPIO
1993 VIRGO / 16.10 LIBRA
1994 SCORPIO
1995 LIBRA / 10.10 SCORPIO
1996 LEO / 5.10 VIRGO
1997 SCORPIO / 8.10 SAGITTARIUS
1998 VIRGO / 2.10 LIBRA
1999 VIRGO / 9.10 LEO
2000 LIBRA / 25.9 SCORPIO
2001 LEO / 5.10 VIRGO
2002 SCORPIO / 8.10 SAGITTARIUS
2003 LIBRA / 10.10 SCORPIO
2004 LEO / 5.10 VIRGO
2005 SCORPIO / 8.10 SAGITTARIUS
2006 VIRGO / 2.10 LIBRA
2007 VIRGO / 9.10 LEO
2008 LIBRA / 25.9 SCORPIO
2009 LEO / 5.10 VIRGO
2010 SCORPIO / 8.10 SAGITTARIUS
2011 LIBRA / 10.10 SCORPIO
2012 LEO / 5.10 VIRGO
2013 SCORPIO / 8.10 SAGITTARIUS
2014 VIRGO / 2.10 LIBRA
2015 VIRGO / 9.10 LEO
2016 SCORPIO / 19.10 SAGITTARIUS
2017 LEO / 5.10 VIRGO
2018 SCORPIO/ 8.10 SAGITTARIUS
2019 LIBRA/ 10.10 SCORPIO

VENUS THROUGH THE ZODIAC SIGNS

Venus in Aries

Amongst other things, the position of Venus in Aries indicates a fondness for travel, music and all creative pursuits. Your nature tends to be affectionate and you would try not to create confusion or difficulty for others if it could be avoided. Many people with this planetary position have a great love of the theatre, and mental stimulation is of the greatest importance. Early romantic attachments are common with Venus in Aries, so it is very important to establish a genuine sense of romantic continuity. Early marriage is not recommended, especially if it is based on sympathy. You may give your heart a little too readily on occasions.

Venus in Taurus

You are capable of very deep feelings and your emotions tend to last for a very long time. This makes you a trusting partner and lover, whose constancy is second to none. In life you are precise and careful and always try to do things the right way. Although this means an ordered life, which you are comfortable with, it can also lead you to be rather too fussy for your own good. Despite your pleasant nature, you are very fixed in your opinions and quite able to speak your mind. Others are attracted to you and historical astrologers always quoted this position of Venus as being very fortunate in terms of marriage. However, if you find yourself involved in a failed relationship, it could take you a long time to trust again.

Venus in Gemini

As with all associations related to Gemini, you tend to be quite versatile, anxious for change and intelligent in your dealings with the world at large. You may gain money from more than one source but you are equally good at spending it. There is an inference here that you are a good communicator, via either the written or the spoken word, and you love to be in the company of interesting people. Always on the look-out for culture, you may also be very fond of music, and love to indulge the curious and cultured side of your nature. In romance you tend to have more than one relationship and could find yourself associated with someone who has previously been a friend or even a distant relative.

Venus in Cancer

You often stay close to home because you are very fond of family and enjoy many of your most treasured moments when you are with those you love. Being naturally sympathetic, you will always do anything you can to support those around you, even people you hardly know at all. This charitable side of your nature is your most noticeable trait and is one of the reasons why others are naturally so fond of you. Being receptive and in some cases even psychic, you can see through to the soul of most of those with whom you come into contact. You may not commence too many romantic attachments but when you do give your heart, it tends to be unconditionally.

Venus in Leo

It must become quickly obvious to almost anyone you meet that you are kind, sympathetic and yet determined enough to stand up for anyone or anything that is truly important to you. Bright and sunny, you warm the world with your natural enthusiasm and would rarely do anything to hurt those around you, or at least not intentionally. In romance you are ardent and sincere, though some may find your style just a little overpowering. Gains come through your contacts with other people and this could be especially true with regard to romance, for love and money often come hand in hand for those who were born with Venus in Leo. People claim to understand you, though you are more complex than you seem.

Venus in Virgo

Your nature could well be fairly quiet no matter what your Sun sign might be, though this fact often manifests itself as an inner peace and would not prevent you from being basically sociable. Some delays and even the odd disappointment in love cannot be ruled out with this planetary position, though it's a fact that you will usually find the happiness you look for in the end. Catapulting yourself into romantic entanglements that you know to be rather ill-advised is not sensible, and it would be better to wait before you committed yourself exclusively to any one person. It is the essence of your nature to serve the world at large and through doing so it is possible that you will attract money at some stage in your life.

Venus in Libra

Venus is very comfortable in Libra and bestows upon those people who have this planetary position a particular sort of kindness that is easy to recognise. This is a very good position for all sorts of friendships and also for romantic attachments that usually bring much joy into your life. Few individuals with Venus in Libra would avoid marriage and since you are capable of great depths of love, it is likely that you will find a contented personal life. You like to mix with people of integrity and intelligence but don't take kindly to scruffy surroundings or work that means getting your hands too dirty. Careful speculation, good business dealings and money through marriage all seem fairly likely.

Venus in Scorpio

You are quite open and tend to spend money quite freely, even on those occasions when you don't have very much. Although your intentions are always good, there are times when you get yourself in to the odd scrape and this can be particularly true when it comes to romance, which you may come to late or from a rather unexpected direction. Certainly you have the power to be happy and to make others contented on the way, but you find the odd stumbling block on your journey through life and it could seem that you have to work harder than those around you. As a result of this, you gain a much deeper understanding of the true value of personal happiness than many people ever do, and are likely to achieve true contentment in the end.

Venus in Sagittarius

You are lighthearted, cheerful and always able to see the funny side of any situation. These facts enhance your popularity, which is especially high with members of the opposite sex. You should never have to look too far to find romantic interest in your life, though it is just possible that you might be too willing to commit yourself before you are certain that the person in question is right for you. Part of the problem here extends to other areas of life too. The fact is that you like variety in everything and so can tire of situations that fail to offer it. All the same, if you choose wisely and learn to understand your restless side, then great happiness can be yours.

Venus in Capricorn

The most notable trait that comes from Venus in this position is that it makes you trustworthy and able to take on all sorts of responsibilities in life. People are instinctively fond of you and love you all the more because you are always ready to help those who are in any form of need. Social and business popularity can be yours and there is a magnetic quality to your nature that is particularly attractive in a romantic sense. Anyone who wants a partner for a lover, a spouse and a good friend too would almost certainly look in your direction. Constancy is the hallmark of your nature and unfaithfulness would go right against the grain. You might sometimes be a little too trusting.

Venus in Aquarius

This location of Venus offers a fondness for travel and a desire to try out something new at every possible opportunity. You are extremely easy to get along with and tend to have many friends from varied backgrounds, classes and inclinations. You like to live a distinct sort of life and gain a great deal from moving about, both in a career sense and with regard to your home. It is not out of the question that you could form a romantic attachment to someone who comes from far away or be attracted to a person of a distinctly artistic and original nature. What you cannot stand is jealousy, for you have friends of both sexes and would want to keep things that way.

Venus in Pisces

The first thing people tend to notice about you is your wonderful, warm smile. Being very charitable by nature you will do anything to help others, even if you don't know them well. Much of your life may be spent sorting out situations for other people, but it is very important to feel that you are living for yourself too. In the main, you remain cheerful, and tend to be quite attractive to members of the opposite sex. Where romantic attachments are concerned, you could be drawn to people who are significantly older or younger than yourself or to someone with a unique career or point of view. It might be best for you to avoid marrying whilst you are still very young.

LIBRA:
2018 DIARY PAGES

♎ October 2018

1 MONDAY
Moon Age Day 22   Moon Sign Gemini

Today could be a time of deep insight and you may have the feeling that life is laid out for you in a much clearer way than is sometimes the case. You can help loved ones in practical ways and this ability also extends to work, where colleagues will be more than pleased to accept your advice and your willingness to pitch in.

2 TUESDAY
Moon Age Day 23   Moon Sign Cancer

You need to seek the wide blue yonder and a late holiday won't be out of the question for some Librans around this time. Even if you can't get away for a lengthy break perhaps you could take a few hours out to do whatever takes your fancy. What will rankle at the moment is having to do what others tell you.

3 WEDNESDAY
Moon Age Day 24   Moon Sign Cancer

It's great to travel, especially if you are a Libran. Take off on a little adventure if you get the chance. You certainly won't do yourself any good at all by sticking around at home all the time and present planetary trends virtually demand a change of scenery. Intellectual pastimes are the most rewarding ones in which to indulge.

4 THURSDAY
Moon Age Day 25   Moon Sign Leo

As usual you will be perpetually on the go and also as normal you will positively hate any sort of routine you see as outmoded and boring. Make use of your natural sense of what's right and dress to impress when you get the chance. This can be especially important in professional settings or for a social function.

5 FRIDAY
Moon Age Day 26   Moon Sign Leo

You work best when you are free to make your own decisions today – a trend that has been obvious for quite some time. It really is too much to expect you to toe any line you don't care for and you could be quite cross if you discover that you have no choice in the matter. Try to stay cool, calm and collected as much as you can today.

6 SATURDAY
Moon Age Day 27   Moon Sign Virgo

Today you are very candid and will brush aside any tendency on the part of others to take over your life. It looks as though this is a recurring theme but things will change significantly in only a few days. Continue to do all you can to welcome newcomers into your social circle because new friends can be made.

7 SUNDAY
Moon Age Day 28   Moon Sign Virgo

Look out for important news, some of which is likely to come from rather surprising directions. There are pointers to your future if you watch what is happening in your immediate vicinity and no job is beneath your dignity today if you think it will impress someone or achieve a desired objective. Libra is fully positive.

8 MONDAY
Moon Age Day 29   Moon Sign Virgo

In personal relationships you can now be slightly provocative, though you are also quite fascinating and people will be happy to have you around. Lively discussions are likely all day long and with a number of different types of people. Avoid constant attention to detail at the moment because it will wear you out.

9 TUESDAY
Moon Age Day 0   Moon Sign Libra

Progress should be easy to achieve today. The lunar high is likely to make you feel brighter, freer and more inclined to take chances. Any sluggish tendencies of the last couple of weeks will disappear and you should be on top form, especially in terms of your social and love life. Stand by for some outrageous possibilities.

10 WEDNESDAY   *Moon Age Day 1   Moon Sign Libra*

The green light is now definitely on and there isn't much that will hold you back once you decide the time is right for action. A little positive thinking goes a very long way under present trends and you have what it takes to impress the most important people in your life. Love shines strongly in your direction, and you reflect it wonderfully.

11 THURSDAY   *Moon Age Day 2   Moon Sign Scorpio*

You will probably have more sympathy for the underdog today and will do all you can to help people who are having problems of one sort or another. You are clearly very concerned for everyone around you and though this is to be praised you might just be doing rather more than you reasonably should in at least one case later today.

12 FRIDAY   *Moon Age Day 3   Moon Sign Scorpio*

Social relationships may be a cause of some frustration right now and you need to be right on form when it comes to the way you speak to people. This isn't at all difficult for Libra as you can be charm itself when you need to be. This is especially important when you are dealing with superiors or people with great influence.

13 SATURDAY   *Moon Age Day 4   Moon Sign Sagittarius*

There is now a more hurried feel to your everyday life and everything seems as though it is happening at the same time. There won't be time right now to get hung up on details and you will be dealing with those matters that can be sorted out and finished in little or no time. Anything complicated should be left for another day.

14 SUNDAY   *Moon Age Day 5   Moon Sign Sagittarius*

Disagreements can arise at home or in almost any situation where you have to follow the lead of people you either don't trust or don't respect. A greater degree of co-operation is called for but don't expect it to be easy now to come to terms with certain people. Part of the trouble is that you are so original yourself.

15 MONDAY   *Moon Age Day 6   Moon Sign Capricorn*

Professionally speaking you could be somewhat overstretched now by someone in authority. At home it is likely that your ability to get on well with others is not quite as obvious today. It could be that you are rebelling against people who are making demands on you that you are not willing to accommodate.

16 TUESDAY   *Moon Age Day 7   Moon Sign Capricorn*

As a rule you hate to be stuck in any sort of routine but this is less likely to be the case under present trends. On the contrary you will take comfort from doing things in the same old way – a fact that might come as a surprise to some of your friends. Don't worry though because even by tomorrow you will be back to normal.

17 WEDNESDAY   *Moon Age Day 8   Moon Sign Capricorn*

A phase of strong personal magnetism is at hand and today is a period during which it ought to be easier to influence other people than it has been of late. Be determined and you can't go far wrong. At this stage of the week you might be slightly concerned about money, though probably not for very long.

18 THURSDAY   *Moon Age Day 9   Moon Sign Aquarius*

There seems to be no way of getting ahead today that doesn't mean doing what someone else wants you to do. This definitely goes against the grain but will prove to be necessary. To refuse to take part would be to cut off your nose to spite your face. Of course you can be stubborn but that won't do you any good at all.

19 FRIDAY   *Moon Age Day 10   Moon Sign Aquarius*

Now you appear to be very career-oriented and will want to put as much energy as possible into getting ahead professionally. You excel at managing or supervising others, even if you have not been earmarked to do so. It's just that at present you are a natural leader and you can't avoid taking control.

20 SATURDAY   *Moon Age Day 11   Moon Sign Pisces*

If you are clever, you can be extremely persuasive today and can get more or less everything you want without having to put in too much in the way of hard, physical work. Socially speaking you seem to be on top form and have what it takes to show yourself in a very favourable light when it matters the most.

21 SUNDAY   *Moon Age Day 12   Moon Sign Pisces*

It is towards the practical world that you can now look for some genuine support. Some of your plans need slightly more than thought and you may have to put in some real effort to get over a particular hurdle. On the way you can find moments of real fun, most likely in the company of people you think of as being your best friends.

22 MONDAY   *Moon Age Day 13   Moon Sign Pisces*

Your role in group activities seems to be highlighted now. You will be feeling distinctly optimistic, willing to fall in line with any reasonable request and you are flexible enough to change your direction at a moment's notice. Give yourself a pat on the back for a success that is a direct result of your hard work.

23 TUESDAY   *Moon Age Day 14   Moon Sign Aries*

The lunar low this month gives you an ideal opportunity to overcome difficulties and achieve your objectives. It's true that there are circumstances that might seem at first to hold you back but you also have a strong determination and a sense of purpose. One thing at once is the best adage; so don't crowd your schedule too much.

24 WEDNESDAY   *Moon Age Day 15   Moon Sign Aries*

You could feel a little cut off from life in some ways but there is a great deal of personal choice about this and you will probably feel quite happy to spend at least some time on your own. It might be difficult to do when you are surrounded by noise and activity, but think things through. Libra is very pensive today.

25 THURSDAY
Moon Age Day 16   Moon Sign Taurus

A little discontent could arise in personal attachments, even though this is more or less forced upon you by circumstances. For this reason alone you are less likely to be spending a great deal of time thinking about romance and will be inclined to dwell more in the practical world. You are likely to be thinking a lot about money.

26 FRIDAY
Moon Age Day 17   Moon Sign Taurus

This should be a fantastic period for putting new plans into action. With everything to play for and a feeling of great confidence, you can now put the finishing touch to something that has been waiting for quite a while. What is most noticeable about today is the way you are able to manipulate situations to suit your own needs.

27 SATURDAY
Moon Age Day 18   Moon Sign Gemini

Look to friends for both support and fulfilment. Whether you realise it or not you are coming to the end of one particular phase in your life and new things need to be allowed in. There's no problem about this as far as you are concerned and you should be quite willing to wear almost any sort of clothes on your journey to better times.

28 SUNDAY
Moon Age Day 19   Moon Sign Gemini

Opportunities that present themselves today probably won't come again for quite a while so focus fully on life. The need to pay attention means you should concentrate on one thing at a time – never an easy task for Libra. You should now be more inclined to analyse your past efforts with a desire to improve.

29 MONDAY
Moon Age Day 20   Moon Sign Cancer

Your vitality, natural sense of fun and your charm are likely to make you popular with most people. The odd person who doesn't care for you all that much can now be ignored because you are too busy to acknowledge them. This would be a great time to join new groups or clubs but do make sure you are not just doing so on a whim.

30 TUESDAY   *Moon Age Day 21   Moon Sign Cancer*

What you are looking at now is great potential for personal growth. Lessons can be learned from situations that are winding down now, or which have come to a logical pause. When you apply yourself to them again or start something new, you will have gained a great deal in terms of experience and contentment.

31 WEDNESDAY   *Moon Age Day 22   Moon Sign Cancer*

It looks as though you are going to be very plain spoken in your dealings with others, especially at work. You won't take no for an answer on those occasions when you are certain of your ground and you seem to be at your most dynamic professionally. At home you will be more relaxed but will still have very definite opinions.

November 2018

1 THURSDAY
Moon Age Day 23   Moon Sign Leo

Making certain dreams into realities now becomes possible, though a little extra effort will be necessary to make the procedure work well. Whether or not you will still want what you desired once it becomes possible, remains to be seen. It is very important to be specific about your requirements in the days and weeks ahead.

2 FRIDAY
Moon Age Day 24   Moon Sign Leo

Your career should prove to be the most important, and possibly also the most interesting, sphere of your life today. Not that you are also lacking when it comes to having a good time. Your ability to mix business with pleasure has probably never been so well developed and it is possible to make good friends from colleagues.

3 SATURDAY
Moon Age Day 25   Moon Sign Virgo

It looks as though your popularity is going to be a major issue. It is possible that you are trying too hard, which really isn't necessary. Just relax and be yourself. When it comes to romance you are likely to be right in the swing of things and showing just how sexy you are capable of being. Look after the pennies for the moment.

4 SUNDAY
Moon Age Day 26   Moon Sign Virgo

Involve yourself as much as possible in group activities and make sure you get together with people who have similar views to your own. Not that there will be any trouble in adapting to different types, but your greatest successes at the moment are likely to come when there is a strong meeting of minds.

57

5 MONDAY
Moon Age Day 27   Moon Sign Libra

This is the best day of the month to break loose and to do whatever takes your fancy. If your time is your own early this week you will want to spend it having fun in good company. Your amazing capacity for successfully mixing business with pleasure should do you a great deal of good at the same time.

6 TUESDAY
Moon Age Day 28   Moon Sign Libra

A high degree of good fortune is likely to attend your life right now and you can make gains by simply being in the right place and by following your intuition. Money matters should take a turn for the better, even if it is only a case of sorting things out in your own mind. Most important of all today is the opportunity to enjoy yourself.

7 WEDNESDAY
Moon Age Day 0   Moon Sign Scorpio

Your career ambitions should be running well, though probably below the surface just for the moment. You sense that superiors are studying you carefully and you will need to give of your best, working quietly but confidently between now and the weekend. Once you are away from work there could be some surprises in store.

8 THURSDAY
Moon Age Day 1   Moon Sign Scorpio

As far as relationships are concerned at this time love matches can be a way to expand your personal horizons and to learn more about life in general. Not that you are restricting yourself in terms of the people you mix with. On the contrary you are very approachable and as interesting to be with as Libra nearly always turns out to be.

9 FRIDAY
Moon Age Day 2   Moon Sign Sagittarius

Life can be a constant learning process and this is certainly the case for the typical Libran. Don't assume today that you know everything about any topic. There are always going to be people who can tell you something new and the more you pay attention the greater will be your appreciation of life's nuances.

10 SATURDAY   *Moon Age Day 3   Moon Sign Sagittarius*

Family matters are accentuated today. You can benefit from the comforts of home and also from activities that are taking place there. There are strong emotional ties at work in your thinking and you will not make many decisions today without seeking the advice of your partner or family members who always offer sound counsel.

11 SUNDAY   *Moon Age Day 4   Moon Sign Sagittarius*

Expect career boosts to be coming along at any time now, though of course probably not on a Sunday. Nevertheless you can do yourself some professional good by thinking through your strategy for next week. You may also be very drawn towards sport under present trends and will be happy to test yourself in some way.

12 MONDAY   *Moon Age Day 5   Moon Sign Capricorn*

You are now looking towards higher purposes and such is the complicated working of your mind that at least some other people won't understand you at all. Try to get together with those individuals who are as unique and far-sighted as you are. Your confidence to do the right thing in relationships is clearly growing now.

13 TUESDAY   *Moon Age Day 6   Moon Sign Capricorn*

It's time to discover the new or the unusual that exists all around you. How exciting life can be and how keen you are to know everything about it. You thrive best when you are educating yourself about the world and that is certainly something you tend to do at this time. New starts at work may be beneficial in the longer-term.

14 WEDNESDAY   *Moon Age Day 7   Moon Sign Aquarius*

Contentious matters are likely to arise and you may find it difficult to get away from issues you would rather ignore altogether. In a personal sense you seem to be making a good impression on someone you find attractive and you might also discover you have an admirer you didn't suspect. Whether that pleases you remains to be seen.

15 THURSDAY *Moon Age Day 8   Moon Sign Aquarius*

Independence and anything unusual are both issues for today. Routine is not a word you want to hear for the moment and you will value anyone who is as 'off the wall' as you are at times. Keep up the good work when it comes to projecting your image on to a bigger and bigger audience and do all you can to be heard.

16 FRIDAY *Moon Age Day 9   Moon Sign Aquarius*

It's just possible that a social contact on which you are inclined to rely may well be missing for now and perhaps the foreseeable future. This might mean having to stand on your own feet. The lessons learned are positive for you because necessity is the mother of invention. You learn some important facts about yourself.

17 SATURDAY ☿ *Moon Age Day 10   Moon Sign Pisces*

This could be one of your most pleasurable days as far as social trends go and it seems you are more than willing to drop some responsibilities in order to have a good time. This is achieved in the company of people you like to be close to. Some of the compliments that come your way today are disguised but well meant.

18 SUNDAY ☿ *Moon Age Day 11   Moon Sign Pisces*

This can be a very positive sort of Sunday but you need to be as free from restrictions as you can manage. There may be people around who seem to hold you back and prevent you from making the progress you would wish. In the 'seesaw' environment you inhabit just at present, it is important to keep trying to break away.

19 MONDAY ☿ *Moon Age Day 12   Moon Sign Aries*

If you are tired today you can at least partly blame the lunar low. This might not be the most dynamic period of the year but it can be warm and comfortable, with much to recommend it in a personal sense. Recognise that people are on your side and the best sort of reassurance is not likely to be far away.

20 TUESDAY ☿ *Moon Age Day 13 Moon Sign Aries*

This is likely to be another day that lacks some of the sparkle you are always seeking but you can still enjoy yourself if you don't have too many expectations. Rules and regulations could easily bother you and although you feel most secure at home you could even feel somewhat tied down there. A few small excursions might help.

21 WEDNESDAY ☿ *Moon Age Day 14 Moon Sign Taurus*

You may have conflicts today with people you re close to. Try to avoid getting embroiled in disputes that can't really help and will only actually hinder your progress. Differences of opinion, though inevitable, can be sorted out rationally. In terms of cash you could discover you are slightly better off than you thought.

22 THURSDAY ☿ *Moon Age Day 15 Moon Sign Taurus*

Whilst it seems plain that your nearest and dearest have your best interests at heart, you could still be having a little trouble with the way they go about trying to help you. Librans are independently minded at this stage and there is little of nothing you can do to redress this balance. Everything should settle down by tomorrow.

23 FRIDAY ☿ *Moon Age Day 16 Moon Sign Taurus*

Now you should find far more beneficial social trends developing, together with a better reaction on your part to the fact that your partner is so keen to get involved in aspects of your life they might have ignored before. Think seriously about an offer that has come in regarding your work and you might just opt for change.

24 SATURDAY ☿ *Moon Age Day 17 Moon Sign Gemini*

Your focus at this time tends to be mainly towards career or practical jobs if you do not work. At home you will also find yourself pretty well committed to getting things done and you tend to be very efficient in the way you manage your time. Look out for the odd sprain or strain – probably brought about by trying too hard physically.

25 SUNDAY ☿ *Moon Age Day 18   Moon Sign Gemini*

Personal relationships could be subject to a few misunderstandings so work hard to resolve these early in the day if they do arise. Compromises at this time can lead to a smoother life and you will feel much better about everything if you get on well with those around you. Look out for an unexpected gain.

26 MONDAY ☿ *Moon Age Day 19   Moon Sign Cancer*

This is one of those days on which you can never be sure what you can learn if you keep your eyes and ears open. Even the most casual of conversations can lead you to understanding something that was a total mystery to you before and you have what it takes to make failure into glorious victory. Things are starting to look good.

27 TUESDAY ☿ *Moon Age Day 20   Moon Sign Cancer*

You will now get more than a little help from your friends and there are plenty of positive highlights surrounding social occasions. Of course there is also time for work but you are even turning this into a joy and mixing it with friendship and compromise. The world is now starting to see the very best of what Libra can be.

28 WEDNESDAY ☿ *Moon Age Day 21   Moon Sign Leo*

You may be feeling a little stale about certain aspects of your life and a Libran desire to change things comes upon you once again. That's fine but don't throw out the baby with the bathwater. Some things are tried and tested and need to stay as they are in order to offer you greater security. It's just a case of working out what to do.

29 THURSDAY ☿ *Moon Age Day 22   Moon Sign Leo*

Though much is moving forward in your life around now, there could be a feeling that you have forgotten something important. Put aside a little time to try and work out what it might be but don't go mad because you could just as easily be suffering from a slight bout of insecurity. In the main, life should now be going your way.

30 FRIDAY ☿ *Moon Age Day 23   Moon Sign Virgo*

You would prefer nothing to hold you back at present, though life rarely works that way and, in any case, some kickback sharpens your intellect and makes you think more deeply. Having to struggle to get your point across is useful, though you could stand a chance of falling into a trap of your own making if you are not careful.

December
2018

1 SATURDAY   ☿   *Moon Age Day 24*   *Moon Sign Virgo*

Be a little careful right now because your emotional suggestibility is at its highest. Right now you tend to believe exactly what you want to believe and that can be something of a mistake. People are generally kind, but there could be the odd selfish individual and that is the one you need to watch out for.

2 SUNDAY   ☿   *Moon Age Day 25*   *Moon Sign Libra*

A result of the enthusiasm you invest in all matters, a little good fortune should now be coming your way. Although this probably won't be anything major it will be important to you and can pave the way to greater successes later on. Give some time to your partner and find ways to have fun that you have not tried before.

3 MONDAY   ☿   *Moon Age Day 26*   *Moon Sign Libra*

Now you should be overflowing with ideas and more willing than ever to test your luck. There should be plenty going on around you in a social sense and you will want to do all you can to make the most of new situations and positive meetings. Give yourself time later in the day to show your concern for family members.

4 TUESDAY   ☿   *Moon Age Day 27*   *Moon Sign Scorpio*

Your chief ability at work now is likely to be your ability to establish contact with other people on an intense level. Communication is now the key to success. There isn't anything particularly unusual about this fact as far as you are concerned but it is the depth of the ties you establish that are proving to be so important at this time.

5 WEDNESDAY ☿ *Moon Age Day 28 Moon Sign Scorpio*

In a professional sense you are best suited to a situation in which you have contact with any number of other people. In this way you can use many of your ideas and you actively need the response that these bring. It is quite likely that some unexpected assistance will come along at some time during today.

6 THURSDAY ☿ *Moon Age Day 29 Moon Sign Scorpio*

A slightly slower and more studied approach to plans and objectives seems to be in order around this time. Keep to one or two simple priorities and try not to crowd your schedule more than is absolutely necessary. In addition to being busy in a practical sense it may only now have occurred to you now that Christmas is getting closer

7 FRIDAY *Moon Age Day 0 Moon Sign Sagittarius*

Your own drives and feelings might be slightly at odds with those of the people you are mixing with most freely. This means there is the possibility of a disagreement you could quite easily do without at this time. It would be better under most circumstances today to withdraw from any issue that looks as though it might get out of control.

8 SATURDAY *Moon Age Day 1 Moon Sign Sagittarius*

You are clearly eager to make a good impression and to get on well with just about everyone. That's fine but it may not be possible under all circumstances. Some people seem determined to be awkward and you may have to disagree with them. However, this doesn't mean your popularity is going to disappear overnight, or at all.

9 SUNDAY *Moon Age Day 2 Moon Sign Capricorn*

Watch out because there might be some unrealistic fantasies to deal with today, mainly coming from the direction of your friends or perhaps family members. On the plus side the romantic possibilities look especially intriguing and potentially rewarding now.

10 MONDAY   *Moon Age Day 3   Moon Sign Capricorn*

It looks as though you will be quite attached to your work at this time and you won't take kindly to anyone trying to pull the professional rug from under you. Your ideas now tend to be creative and progress and decisions you make at this time ought to show very good judgement. Treat the secrets of your friends with great respect.

11 TUESDAY   *Moon Age Day 4   Moon Sign Aquarius*

True to your fun loving Libran nature you function best at the moment when you are involved in a team or some sort of social group. Whether you are working or simply finding ways to have fun this should turn out to be an eventful and generally rewarding day.

12 WEDNESDAY   *Moon Age Day 5   Moon Sign Aquarius*

Right now you are very impressionable and will be easily influenced by others. There's nothing wrong with this just as long as you are aware that not everyone is as honest or decent as you are. There could be times today when you will be happy to withdraw.

13 THURSDAY   *Moon Age Day 6   Moon Sign Aquarius*

In a social sense it looks as though trends continue to be very favourable. Groups of people provide the greatest stimulus at the moment and your general motto seems to be 'the more the merrier'. Parties will be forthcoming and gatherings with the sort of people who give you good ideas. Mixing and mingling is now second nature.

14 FRIDAY   *Moon Age Day 7   Moon Sign Pisces*

What happens today in personal relationships might be far from inspiring – at least at first. However, you should not underestimate your own ability to bring people round to your point of view. With a little determination and plenty of Libran know-how you can work wonders. Keep an eye on money right now.

15 SATURDAY   *Moon Age Day 8   Moon Sign Pisces*

The accent today seems to be on the domestic scene and you will have plenty of time to concentrate on making your nearest and dearest happy. All the same, you don't want life to become dull and you might find ways to integrate family members into your busy social scene. Librans who are studying should be doing fine.

16 SUNDAY   *Moon Age Day 9   Moon Sign Pisces*

Today the major focus needs to be on having fun. Even when you are doing the most mundane of jobs you can find ways to make them seem more exciting and you can also inspire others to do things for you. The general path of life at the moment is towards greater success, even if there are a few diversions on the way.

17 MONDAY   *Moon Age Day 10   Moon Sign Aries*

Some of your plans for today might have to be altered at the last minute but the way to deal with the odd difficult situation is to react by instinct – something you are very good at doing. You won't feel the need to travel now and will probably enjoy a stay-at-home sort of Monday if that proves to be possible.

18 TUESDAY   *Moon Age Day 11   Moon Sign Aries*

Perhaps you will be slightly quieter for the moment and if this is the case you can thank the presence of the Moon in your opposite zodiac sign. This is a state of affairs that you deal with every month and it is intended to be a time to plan for more progressive times. Take time out to contact a distant friend.

19 WEDNESDAY   *Moon Age Day 12   Moon Sign Taurus*

Your social skills are now increased and in the roller-coaster ride that is life at the moment you are now on your way to the top again. Your ability to make a good impression on people you see as being important has rarely been better than it is at present. Use today to do some of those important jobs at home.

20 THURSDAY · *Moon Age Day 13   Moon Sign Taurus*

Some slight setbacks at the start of today should not be allowed to stop you from moving forward in a generally positive way. Try not to restrict yourself to your own four walls around now but get out and meet people whenever and wherever possible. A few new tricks on your part make for a fun time today.

21 FRIDAY · *Moon Age Day 14   Moon Sign Gemini*

New meetings with others can inspire you to come up with good ideas and you are certainly not likely to slow down the practical and positive side of life just to accommodate the festive season. On the contrary, you might even shelve one or two aspects of Christmas planning in order to pursue something you see as important.

22 SATURDAY · *Moon Age Day 15   Moon Sign Gemini*

This is a time to realise how good your love life can be and a period when it is possible to take a short holiday from the responsibilities that might have been pressing in on you for a while. Socially speaking the trends are excellent and it looks as though the Christmas bug has bitten you at last, even though you held out well.

23 SUNDAY · *Moon Age Day 16   Moon Sign Cancer*

Although this is the start of the festive season and therefore a generally optimistic period as far as you are concerned, there is a slight risk that you will lose your sense of proportion in some situations. Try not to worry and certainly don't dwell upon what might go wrong. In the main, you should find this to be a mostly successful day.

24 MONDAY · *Moon Age Day 17   Moon Sign Cancer*

Christmas Eve trends favour a quick and accurate assessment of life's possibilities, plus an insatiable desire to see and do as much as you can. No matter what the weather is doing you will probably want to get out of doors and enjoy the fresh air and you will be quite sure of all your views and opinions at this time.

25 TUESDAY
Moon Age Day 18   Moon Sign Leo

Christmas Day finds you optimistic, keen to get out and about and simply bursting to show an unsuspecting world what you are capable of doing. Planetary assistance comes at a most opportune time and it encourages you to leave your own domain and go visiting. Challenges are taken on board willingly and dealt with excellently.

26 WEDNESDAY
Moon Age Day 19   Moon Sign Leo

This turns out to be an extremely good time for problem solving. Perhaps take a day out from most of the celebrations, and put your mind to the test. This is always a good exercise for you, though you should not make more out of your findings than is really present. Confidence and optimism remain high.

27 THURSDAY
Moon Age Day 20   Moon Sign Virgo

It is quite likely that the period between now and the New Year will be one of movement and merriment. You will be settling to what is expected of you during the holiday break and making the most of the social trends that are looking so good. You may even make the odd financial gain today.

28 FRIDAY
Moon Age Day 21   Moon Sign Virgo

This is going to be a great time for social gatherings, at home or at work. Your mind turns away from the practical and towards having fun. What really sets today apart is your popularity and how much you can influence the lives of some people who may not have been going through a good time of late.

29 SATURDAY
Moon Age Day 22   Moon Sign Libra

Certain situations are apt to disappear from your life at this time, though most of them are going to be things you are quite happy – even overjoyed – to leave behind. You are on a generally upward trend and today brings you closer to your heart's desire in ways that have little or nothing to do with the festivities.

30 SUNDAY   *Moon Age Day 23   Moon Sign Libra*

Unhealthy habits can be easy to shake off, even though this is generally a part of the year during which excess rules. You are feeling fitter and healthier than has been the case and that makes you want to chase the ideals of perfection that are always in your mind. A reflection of this is just how much others think about you now.

31 MONDAY   *Moon Age Day 24   Moon Sign Libra*

Only you can decide how today is going to go, which infers some responsibility. This doesn't trouble you in the slightest because you should be feeling fitter and more confident than ever. This New Year's Eve, consider the things you need to leave behind, even if many of them are trivial. Have some fun tonight.

LIBRA:
2019 DIARY PAGES

LIBRA:
YOUR YEAR IN BRIEF

January and February may not exactly offer you your heart's desire in every sense but both are likely to be above average months in terms of general good luck. It seems that you will have the bit between your teeth in a professional sense and you know how to get what you want even when you are at home. What is even better is that you do all of this whilst at the same time showing how charming you can be.

March and April should prove to be very eventful and might lead to a better understanding of issues that have been on your mind for some time. You think clearly and act positively – so much so that others may rely on you, while at the same time offering you support. Your love life should be very interesting at this time and some new starts may replace disappointments from the past.

With more and more things likely to be turning your way, May and June seem to work very much in your favour. The Sun is gradually moving on and the more it does so the easier it is for you to see your way ahead. Of course not everything will be going your way. Jealousy may be the motivation behind people who don't appear to want you to succeed. Recognise this, don't over-react, and all should be well.

High summer sees you in your element and giving your best to everything. This is a time of year you love and you sparkle like the Sun itself as you make the most of all that's on offer during July and August. Travel is likely, especially by air, and you revel in the company of people who are not only charming but who turn out to be extremely useful to your long-term plans.

As the hottest days of the year retreat into the background, so you settle back into something like a routine – although perhaps from a new vantage point. September and October should be good months for making domestic choices and for bringing relationships up-to-date in a way that hasn't been possible earlier in the year. You won't allow anyone who disagrees with you to disturb your equilibrium.

The last two months of the year, November and December look set to be a time of social change and personal contentment. You are often particular about the way you want life to be but this is less evident under present trends. An easy-going attitude causes you to worry less and this reflects in your relationships with others. Make Christmas special for family members and friends, and be the life and soul of the party. Surprisingly, trends point to you making your New Year resolutions with fingers firmly crossed!

January 2019

1 TUESDAY
Moon Age Day 25   Moon Sign Scorpio

Intimate relationships are what make life interesting at the start of this new year. Stand up for what you know to be right in professional attachments, and let the one you love know how important they are to you. A small present or a kind word could help to create a loving mood, but what's most important now is to offer reassurance.

2 WEDNESDAY
Moon Age Day 26   Moon Sign Scorpio

A fruitful phase in the monetary sphere has arrived, making this a time when you will not willingly miss out what you see as important events. In addition, anything old, unusual or curious is likely to appeal to you. Later in the day, your thoughts may turn towards the days that lie ahead and the plans that you can make for them.

3 THURSDAY
Moon Age Day 27   Moon Sign Sagittarius

Getting on with others in group situations might be quite difficult today, which is why you may prefer to stick to one-to-one encounters. This will not be possible all the time and in any case, there are trends around now that you need to counter, rather than trying to pretend they don't exist.

4 FRIDAY
Moon Age Day 28   Moon Sign Sagittarius

Since variety is the spice of life to you, that's what you need to be finding at present. It might not be easy and an extra helping of effort may be needed. Don't allow issues that you can do nothing about to weigh you down but instead concentrate on those matters you can change.

5 SATURDAY — Moon Age Day 0 — Moon Sign Capricorn

Pressure from friends or colleagues is difficult to counter today, especially if what they are saying makes a great deal of sense. Listen, think and then take the sort of action that you know to be right. Once you have made a decision today, stick to it, even if you begin to have some slight doubts later.

6 SUNDAY — Moon Age Day 1 — Moon Sign Capricorn

The way ahead now ought to look much clearer. It's true that there are decisions to be made at present but there should be plenty of people around who are interested enough in your life to offer you invaluable assistance. Conflict in the work place is less likely today and personal attachments may bring happiness in the evening.

7 MONDAY — Moon Age Day 2 — Moon Sign Capricorn

This is another day on which you will want to do something exciting or different. Some extra effort may be needed if you have to wade through reams of red tape but you will not be lacking in confidence, nor the support you require. The only component that might not be present is sufficient time to get everything organised.

8 TUESDAY — Moon Age Day 3 — Moon Sign Aquarius

Trends suggest that career goals are the ones you will be chasing at this stage of the working week. Those closest to you in a professional sense may be in a position to do you some real favours, though you might have to court their favour first. That's no problem because the planets make you quite charming and complimentary to others at present.

9 WEDNESDAY — Moon Age Day 4 — Moon Sign Aquarius

There are compromises to be made today, especially in group situations. That means taking a back seat now and again, not something that appeals to you too much at any time. A general restlessness that has beset you since the beginning of the month is still present, though probably more controlled now.

10 THURSDAY   *Moon Age Day 5   Moon Sign Pisces*

News from far off could prove to be especially heart-warming and this is likely to be a red-letter day in more than one sense of the word. Keep up your efforts to get ahead at work, but also enjoy the social trends that are looking so good for you at present. An inspirational new idea stands a chance of working out well.

11 FRIDAY   *Moon Age Day 6   Moon Sign Pisces*

A domestic partner or perhaps a friend may exhibit a degree of inflexibility at present that is quite difficult to counter. In reality, it might not be worth trying. Accept people for what they are and let them get on with the life they want to live, but make sure that their attitude does not rub off on you in any way.

12 SATURDAY   *Moon Age Day 7   Moon Sign Pisces*

If professional obligations have weighed on your mind, it is possible that the weekend will give you a break. There is no reason to assume that a couple of quieter days will cause you any real problem in the longer term and people should be more than willing to put themselves out on your behalf at almost any stage today.

13 SUNDAY   *Moon Age Day 8   Moon Sign Aries*

It is time to take things steadily and to keep your expectations to a minimum. It isn't that you fail to make progress, merely that you are slowed down. Luckily, this is Sunday so there is a greater chance that you can take things easily for a while at least today. Spend a few hours in the company of those who love you.

14 MONDAY   *Moon Age Day 9   Moon Sign Aries*

Gradually you should begin to feel more like your usual self by the end of the day you could find that you have got a good deal done. Contradictions are likely, particularly in terms of the way people are behaving at work, though you should be quite glad to be back in harness and won't have too much difficulty getting on with people.

15 TUESDAY
Moon Age Day 10   Moon Sign Taurus

You may now feel drawn to the practical side of life and have the right sort of mental ammunition to take on any job. Trends indicate that there will be a few outstanding issues that have to be addressed, even if to do so is quite hard and maybe a little depressing. You can get where you need to be, but accept that it will take time right now.

16 WEDNESDAY
Moon Age Day 11   Moon Sign Taurus

There is a much more co-operative atmosphere about today and you should be pleased to find that you are getting on well with people who haven't been that easy to come to terms with in the past. Although you have a good deal on your plate, you undertake most jobs with a smile on your face.

17 THURSDAY
Moon Age Day 12   Moon Sign Taurus

Much of what happens in personal relationships at present can really surprise you. It looks as though you will be in the good books of people whose approval may be influential your life. This is especially true at work, where your original and even inspirational ways are being carefully observed.

18 FRIDAY
Moon Age Day 13   Moon Sign Gemini

It might be difficult to please certain people at present, which might mean that as a result you avoid trying to do so. It is important to keep your temper because the people you might fall out with today are the ones you may need to rely on later. If something upsets you, try to shrug your shoulders and turn your attention elsewhere.

19 SATURDAY
Moon Age Day 14   Moon Sign Gemini

Under present trends, many Librans will feel mentally strong to the point where they are unbeatable, most noticeably at work. Remember the old adage, 'pride comes before a fall'. Remain modest and humble enough to admit to yourself and to those around you that there will always be someone who knows better than you.

YOUR DAILY GUIDE TO JANUARY 2019

20 SUNDAY   *Moon Age Day 15   Moon Sign Cancer*

You could be in a better position than usual to influence the throw of the dice as far as general good luck is concerned. Meanwhile, others, some of whom have great influence, may notice your sunny disposition. Certainly in professional sense it should be noted that it's not what you know but who you know that counts right now.

21 MONDAY   *Moon Age Day 16   Moon Sign Cancer*

Look towards opportunities for growth, which should be making themselves very clear around now. The start of the new working week is likely to be busy but you undertake most jobs with a smile. Avoid rushing any task because under present trends it is more likely than usual to lead to a terrible muddle.

22 TUESDAY   *Moon Age Day 17   Moon Sign Leo*

Your ingenuity comes to the rescue when it is most important. It is vital you look at life from all angles at the moment and don't dismiss any possibility until you have studied it carefully. Anything that others find difficult to do is grist to the mill for Libra on this day.

23 WEDNESDAY   *Moon Age Day 18   Moon Sign Leo*

Close and intimate twosomes can make life richer and more interesting at this time. Although trends suggest that you might be feeling somewhat nervy about something, a warm cuddle can set you back on track. This could be a really interesting time, and the more so if you do things that stimulate your intellect.

24 THURSDAY   *Moon Age Day 19   Moon Sign Virgo*

Your influence is very important right now, if only because people generally are taking so much notice of your opinions. That's why it is vitally important to think things through rationally and not to shoot from the hip. If people in the family are arguing, you can pour oil on troubled water.

25 FRIDAY
Moon Age Day 20   Moon Sign Virgo

You will probably prefer to be on the move whenever you can today. Staying in one place for too long could be boring and might make it difficult for you to concentrate. This is a frame of mind that Libra finds itself in now and again but the way around it is to stay active and interested in what's happening around you.

26 SATURDAY
Moon Age Day 21   Moon Sign Libra

Things are quite clearly going your way today and you may find yourself in a position to influence situations much more than has been the case previously. What matters the most is the impression you make on others, which is strong and enduring at this time. Your buzzy and carefree nature is quite evident to everyone.

27 SUNDAY
Moon Age Day 22   Moon Sign Libra

With targets for your present restless and searching spirit, the lunar high ought to offer you a Sunday that is filled with possibilities. You are joyful, easy to talk to and have everyone's best interests at heart. It could be an exhausting day, but should be very enjoyable too. Not a time to sit and think about things.

28 MONDAY
Moon Age Day 23   Moon Sign Scorpio

Don't fall foul of others in arguments right now because to do so will only complicate your life in ways that are not necessary. Keep it light and simple and walk away from disputes of almost any sort. Although you might be seething inside, in a few hours you will be glad of your adult attitude.

29 TUESDAY
Moon Age Day 24   Moon Sign Scorpio

Today brings a strong emphasis on broadening your horizons; not a bad thing at this stage of the working week, particularly since there should be people around who are willing to lend a hand if you are away. Stay away from unnecessary complications and always look to the easiest way of solving a problem.

30 WEDNESDAY *Moon Age Day 25* *Moon Sign Sagittarius*

Though work and practical affairs should prove to be running smoothly today, the same cannot be said regarding personal attachments and family matters. Trends suggest that the closer you are to someone, the less likely you are to understand what makes them tick. Some serious concentration is called for.

31 THURSDAY *Moon Age Day 26* *Moon Sign Sagittarius*

The most promising area for you today appears to be personal relationships. While it's true that you also favour practical tasks now and are probably feeling light-hearted, you are unlikely to be in the mood for pushing too hard. The bosom of your family looks like the best place to be.

February

2019

1 FRIDAY
Moon Age Day 27   Moon Sign Sagittarius

Whatever new ideas you have up your sleeve are worth putting into action today. There are offers coming in that you might find difficult to refuse and you are likely to have your hands full dealing with one or two wayward friends. All in all, you should be enjoying life, even if some demands are made of you.

2 SATURDAY
Moon Age Day 28   Moon Sign Capricorn

Planetary trends suggest that a social contact or acquaintance might cause a disappointing situation that leaves you running for cover to trusted friends and relatives. Although unusual for Libra, there is a possibility that you are somewhat out of your depth at the moment. Your confidence will return as trends move on.

3 SUNDAY
Moon Age Day 29   Moon Sign Capricorn

You should have improved problem-solving skills today, and it looks as though some of the shine is returning to your sunny nature. Although you won't find everyone easy to get along with, when it matters most you can make the best of impressions. Don't be afraid to tell someone very special how you feel.

4 MONDAY
Moon Age Day 0   Moon Sign Aquarius

This should be a very rewarding time socially, with new opportunities cropping up all the time and the chance to turn business into pleasure. There may be many people virtually lining up to help you out. However, remember to take your time over important tasks, as it will be best to get them right first time.

5 TUESDAY
Moon Age Day 1   Moon Sign Aquarius

There is a chance you might miss something important today, although at the same time you might get an opportunity to turn an apparent disadvantage to your own favour. Rehearse what you are going to say when you know people will be watching, but allow a degree of spontaneity to creep in too.

6 WEDNESDAY
Moon Age Day 2   Moon Sign Aquarius

Your ability to attract new people into your life should be very good at this time. Contrary to the opinions of some, you should find it easy to concentrate and might get the chance to prove it. There may be times later in the day when you can tell your loved one how you really feel about them.

7 THURSDAY
Moon Age Day 3   Moon Sign Pisces

With your ego now a good deal stronger than of late, you have what it takes to forge ahead. Today should be especially good with regard to financial considerations, and your practical common sense is also in evidence. Your intuition works best of all and looks extremely unlikely to let you down.

8 FRIDAY
Moon Age Day 4   Moon Sign Pisces

You are likely to be in a charitable and empathetic mood now, a fact that is hardly likely to be lost on relatives and friends alike. If nothing is happening that takes your fancy at the moment, you will need to apply yourself positively. You can create excitement simply by snapping your fingers and demanding attention.

9 SATURDAY
Moon Age Day 5   Moon Sign Aries

Don't expect to get all your own way this weekend. The lunar low may hold you back a little, though certainly not as much as would sometimes be the case. If you feel you are up against it in terms of the things you have to do, look for some help and support; it will be most welcome during this interlude.

10 SUNDAY
Moon Age Day 6   Moon Sign Aries

A planetary lull patch is in operation, and there really isn't much you can do about it. You could decide to take a rest, of course, which would certainly do you a great deal of good. However, this is not a situation that is very much to your liking and so a degree of Libran patience will be called for today.

11 MONDAY
Moon Age Day 7   Moon Sign Aries

There are influences today that could bring the weird and wonderful into your life. Anything old or unusual will be of interest, to the extent that it may cause comment among your friends and family. The influence won't last long, so do what makes you happy. At least you are making some sort of impression on those around you!

12 TUESDAY
Moon Age Day 8   Moon Sign Taurus

You should be more than happy to form new social contacts today and to also make the most of any new professional opportunity that comes your way. The fresher you are, the better is the impression you will be making, so rest is important too. It's amazing just how much you can get through at this time.

13 WEDNESDAY
Moon Age Day 9   Moon Sign Taurus

The emotional side of life is likely to dominate today. As a result you can be as high as a kite, or in floods of tears; it all depends on the circumstances. Most of these you are creating for yourself and there really isn't any pressure being placed upon you that cannot be ultimately traced to your own attitude.

14 THURSDAY
Moon Age Day 10   Moon Sign Gemini

A change is as good as a rest to Libra at almost any time, but particularly so today. If you get the chance to take a journey, grab it with both hands. However, your creative potential is also strong and you may get the chance to show others this if a trip is not option right now. Don't stack up too much work now because you need some time to relax.

15 FRIDAY   *Moon Age Day 11   Moon Sign Gemini*

There may be some obstacles around today, and trends indicate that these may be at work. Although you are keeping your mind on the job and doing quite well in most situations, you might begin to feel that others are working against your best interests. Consider tackling the situation head-on in the most diplomatic way possible if this is the case.

16 SATURDAY   *Moon Age Day 12   Moon Sign Cancer*

Your day-to-day life should generate more than a few pleasant surprises today and it appears that others are doing more or less everything they can to support you. Social trends are very good so you will want to mix with as many different sorts of people as you can at this time.

17 SUNDAY   *Moon Age Day 13   Moon Sign Cancer*

Whilst you clearly want to satisfy your mental restlessness around this time, there are questions that are going to remain unanswered today. It is possible that people in the know can be especially helpful and there is a distinct possibility that you will be getting on well in a professional sense.

18 MONDAY   *Moon Age Day 14   Moon Sign Leo*

You won't have to try too hard to be in places that are interesting today since most possibilities seem to have their own fascination. Stay away from pointless rules and regulations that can really get on your nerves and don't get involved in any sort of puzzle that begins to occupy you totally.

19 TUESDAY   *Moon Age Day 15   Moon Sign Leo*

There is something weird and wonderful about today but that won't bother you too much. The weird element might come from the behaviour of family and friends, which can surprise you. As for the wonderful, you almost certainly won't have to look any further than your very satisfying love life.

20 WEDNESDAY   *Moon Age Day 16   Moon Sign Virgo*

Yet another astrological trend puts you firmly in touch with the wider world beyond your own door. There is a tendency now to act on impulse but there is nothing especially unusual about this for you. Things could be generally quieter but don't worry because they will liven up in a day or two.

21 THURSDAY   *Moon Age Day 17   Moon Sign Virgo*

Current endeavours should move swiftly towards satisfactory conclusions and today is not without its own sort of excitement. Although not everyone wants to join in the fun, there may be a significant number of people around who do everything they can to be of use to you and who should find you very interesting.

22 FRIDAY   *Moon Age Day 18   Moon Sign Libra*

There is more than a little luck behind today's undertakings so be willing to pitch in and have a go. People seem to be on your side, even on those occasions when true confidence is somewhat lacking on your part. It is in the nature of Libra right now to steam ahead, even into uncharted waters and today proves this.

23 SATURDAY   *Moon Age Day 19   Moon Sign Libra*

The lunar high could put you in a high profile position this time around, and bring plenty of chances to get ahead. This weekend may prove to be the best of the month so be bold and brave, especially when you are dealing with situations you understand. The secret to your success today is your razor sharp intellect and strong intuition.

24 SUNDAY   *Moon Age Day 20   Moon Sign Scorpio*

This may be one of the best days of the month in a personal sense, with romantic possibilities cropping up at every turn. Don't stop pushing ahead in some way towards a longed-for objective but also remember that there is going to be plenty of time to finalise some important plans.

25 MONDAY   *Moon Age Day 21   Moon Sign Scorpio*

Freedom appears to be the key to happiness and it is obvious that you want to seek out wide-open spaces and places where you can feel unfettered. Trends also suggest that someone you haven't seen for quite some time could make a repeat visit to your life, bringing with them a few quite startling surprises.

26 TUESDAY   *Moon Age Day 22   Moon Sign Sagittarius*

Your professional life should be getting better and better, leaving you feeling that you can't put a foot wrong. Take care though! As the saying goes, 'pride goes before a fall' and you won't help yourself if you insist that you are right about everything. Today demands a touch of humility in anything you do.

27 WEDNESDAY   *Moon Age Day 23   Moon Sign Sagittarius*

Your social life continues in a positive vein and you seem to be in no doubt about your place in the world. Whether there will actually be any time to get things done remains in some doubt. Friends should be very supportive at this time and romantic highlights are likely to show themselves throughout the day.

28 THURSDAY   *Moon Age Day 24   Moon Sign Sagittarius*

What happens in relationships around now could put you under a degree of pressure, perhaps because some people are behaving in rather less than typical ways. Most people should be kind, especially acquaintances, and since you have plenty of energy at this time, it looks as though you will enjoy an eventful and even exciting day.

March 2019

1 FRIDAY
Moon Age Day 25   Moon Sign Capricorn

People in authority should be happy to help you at this time and fuel your tanks for the journey along the road towards success. March is likely to bring one or two more problems than you encountered during February, although in the main you should be able to deal with these as and when they arise.

2 SATURDAY
Moon Age Day 26   Moon Sign Capricorn

Don't try to diversify too much at the moment. Being able to do so is one of your strong points, but there are times when it can appear to be a weakness. Concentration on the task in hand is of supreme importance right now, if only because it allows others to know you are consistent. Trends suggest that you should receive a good deal of support as well.

3 SUNDAY
Moon Age Day 27   Moon Sign Aquarius

You may recognise this as a period in which you are being tested, particularly where relationships are concerned. You will need to remain open-minded and fair, particularly when dealing with your life partner. This Sunday should bring some light relief and allow you to put the humorous side of your nature on display.

4 MONDAY
Moon Age Day 28   Moon Sign Aquarius

You should find yourself the centre of attention for much of the time today. With a cheerful attitude and a smile on your face it will be difficult for people not to notice you. When it comes to getting things done the motto is 'slow and steady wins the race', although this won't be easy for Libra at present.

5 TUESDAY   *Moon Age Day 29   Moon Sign Aquarius*

Information coming your way may prove to be quite misleading, so take care to check and re-check things for yourself. Although you have plenty on your plate in a practical sense at the moment, you might decide to spend some time with family members. There are people around who really need your support at present.

6 WEDNESDAY   ☿   *Moon Age Day 0   Moon Sign Pisces*

Weigh up your options carefully today, but once you have made up your mind about a particular course of action, go for it in a big way. You might have to put in some extra effort, but the results will be worth it. All affairs of the heart are highlighted and made that much better under the prevailing astrological trends.

7 THURSDAY   ☿   *Moon Age Day 1   Moon Sign Pisces*

A few financial or practical setbacks are very unlikely to hold you up for any length of time now. The fact is that you are working well, so much so that you could be taking on too much. Plan ahead for journeys that you intend to take later and get a change of scene today if you can.

8 FRIDAY   ☿   *Moon Age Day 2   Moon Sign Aries*

Energy is suddenly in short supply and it has to be said that unless you prepare for this eventuality, the lunar low could take the wind out of your sails. If, on the other hand, you decide right from the start that you will take things easy today, the worst of the potential difficulties can be mitigated altogether.

9 SATURDAY   ☿   *Moon Age Day 3   Moon Sign Aries*

Treat this day as a rest period between activities and instead of trying to move mountains by yourself, call on the help and support of people who care for you. Trends indicate some surprising advantages to be gained later in the day, by which time the worst aspects of the Moon's present position are passing.

10 SUNDAY ☿ *Moon Age Day 4 Moon Sign Taurus*

Your ego suffers a setback today and you may seem to others to be in a humble mood. Actually, this might turn out to be a good thing. Libra can sometimes come across as a little arrogant at times, although this is unintentional. It does no harm at all for the world to see what you really are at heart.

11 MONDAY ☿ *Moon Age Day 5 Moon Sign Taurus*

A talk with a friend or someone whose opinions you value could turn out to be very useful today. The freedom-loving qualities of Air-sign Libra are starting to kick in, leaving you feeling that you want to be on the move. Even if you only manage a shopping trip, it would be better than nothing.

12 TUESDAY ☿ *Moon Age Day 6 Moon Sign Taurus*

It wouldn't be particularly sensible to believe everything you hear today, and especially not when it is obvious that the people making remarks have a vested interest in them. If you need to listen to anyone, choose someone who has nothing to gain but upon whom you can rely to be honest.

13 WEDNESDAY ☿ *Moon Age Day 7 Moon Sign Gemini*

Certain planetary positions indicate that you might be waiting for results of some kind today. Don't allow this to overshadow the day as a whole. Put plans into action and have patience. You won't get anywhere now by rushing anything or by trying to force people down roads they definitely do not want to travel. Keep an open mind regarding family commitments.

14 THURSDAY ☿ *Moon Age Day 8 Moon Sign Gemini*

In terms of feeding your ego, this period could hardly be better. It appears that you will barely have to open your mouth in order for others to applaud your words and your bubbly nature. You may even really like yourself at the moment, which isn't all that common for people born under your zodiac sign.

15 FRIDAY ☿ *Moon Age Day 9 Moon Sign Cancer*

It appears likely that you are now working on collective jobs alongside people with whom you get along well. This Friday ought to be useful, but at the same time fun. If this doesn't turn out to be the case, you will need to alter a few circumstances. It's best to begin with the right ground rules.

16 SATURDAY ☿ *Moon Age Day 10 Moon Sign Cancer*

You may get a great opportunity today to broaden your horizons in some way. Travel and intellectual pursuits of all sorts are likely to appeal to you at the moment and it is clear that the inquisitive side of your nature is on display too. You should discover that family members are being particularly supportive at this time.

17 SUNDAY ☿ *Moon Age Day 11 Moon Sign Cancer*

Things go better now when you are involved in group activities. Libra is not a natural loner and the support that comes from knowing others are on your side is very important. If there is something you have been wanting of late, this might be the very best time to ask for it.

18 MONDAY ☿ *Moon Age Day 12 Moon Sign Leo*

It seems likely that you will be making more than satisfactory progress with your career objectives, and that this sphere of your life is getting a good deal of your attention. Family concerns, if you have any, will have to be left on the back burner for a few hours, though you could find a particular friendship more than helpful this evening.

19 TUESDAY ☿ *Moon Age Day 13 Moon Sign Leo*

There is help around if you want it and even if you don't it is unlikely that you would let anyone know it. You are good to know, inspirational in relationships and warm to your friends. Conversation comes easily to you and this could allow you to address the worries that a friend finds difficult to express.

20 WEDNESDAY ☿ *Moon Age Day 14   Moon Sign Virgo*

You may feel that there are people around today who seem to exist in order to test your patience. The way forward is very clear but difficult to follow so don't rise to the bait. The more calm and collected you remain, the greater is the chance you will bring even the most awkward types around to your point of view.

21 THURSDAY ☿ *Moon Age Day 15   Moon Sign Virgo*

Hold back on important decisions until tomorrow and don't allow yourself to be pushed into anything that goes against the grain. Deferring plans is not the same as cancelling them and it certainly looks likely that you will find things going more smoothly tomorrow. For now, take a well-earned break.

22 FRIDAY ☿ *Moon Age Day 16   Moon Sign Libra*

The Moon is back in your zodiac sign, and not a moment too soon as far as you are concerned. Now you have the chance to show what you are really like. It doesn't matter whether you are trying to clinch a deal or taking part in an activity away from the workplace. Your natural charm shows.

23 SATURDAY ☿ *Moon Age Day 17   Moon Sign Libra*

You ought to be able to get your own way quite easily now. This weekend offers better potential than any time so far this month. This is a time when you need to be in a position to shine in a public arena. No matter how much you have to reorganise things, this is no time to hide your light at all.

24 SUNDAY ☿ *Moon Age Day 18   Moon Sign Scorpio*

There is very little that is beyond your capabilities at the moment, even if the arrival of Sunday turns out to be a mixed blessing. The very best trends right now are geared towards your career, which might be difficult to address if you don't work on a Sunday. Never mind, settle for having a good time instead.

25 MONDAY ☿ *Moon Age Day 19* *Moon Sign Scorpio*

Once again you find yourself at your best if you are involved in group activities of some sort. Don't leave others to sort out details but check everything through carefully yourself. The attitude of loved ones may be difficult to fathom but take into account any age gap differences, or the fact that there may be circumstances you don't know about.

26 TUESDAY ☿ *Moon Age Day 20* *Moon Sign Sagittarius*

Romantic prospects look better for you as the Moon changes its house position. With plenty of love to offer those who are important to you, don't hold back on your Libran ability to find the right words. In practical situations you might need to call upon the help of someone who is definitely in the know.

27 WEDNESDAY ☿ *Moon Age Day 21* *Moon Sign Sagittarius*

The practical side of life may lead to a few difficulties today. This may not be the best time of the month to build a new conservatory or even to decorate the kitchen. What this Wednesday really demands is something away from physical tasks, perhaps out and about, and a concentration on matters that won't lead you to hit your thumb with a hammer!

28 THURSDAY ☿ *Moon Age Day 22* *Moon Sign Capricorn*

There is no sense in trying too hard in directions that are clearly not working. Be selective today and stick to those areas of life that are going according to plan. Spending some time with those you love the most may prove comforting could offer you support through a slightly irritating patch.

29 FRIDAY *Moon Age Day 23* *Moon Sign Capricorn*

Today could see you suffering from a know-it-all attitude, to which Libran people are not usually inclined. It's hard to realise that this is going on but the reactions of others ought to be a good sign. Try to be as humble as you can today and realise that there are always different points of view. Avoid stubborn reactions to issues raised by those around you.

30 SATURDAY   *Moon Age Day 24   Moon Sign Capricorn*

If there is one thing that is really likely to make you enthusiastic at the moment, it is the possibility of travel. You need fresh fields and pastures new and won't be too inclined to stick around the house this Saturday. If, however, you are committed to be somewhere, or are working, it is your fertile imagination that offers the stimulation you need.

31 SUNDAY   *Moon Age Day 25   Moon Sign Aquarius*

When it comes to the social side of life, you are at your very best now. It shouldn't be hard for you to modify your inclinations to suit those of others and to adapt in a moment-by-moment sense. Intellectually speaking, it is clear that you are on top form around this time.

April

2019

1 MONDAY
Moon Age Day 26   Moon Sign Aquarius

Socially speaking you should be on a winning streak all this week, and today is no exception. You will know just the right things to say in order to get others on your side, and you might also be able to look forward to a little more in the way of good luck, at least between now and the middle of the working week.

2 TUESDAY
Moon Age Day 27   Moon Sign Pisces

Your powers of attraction are looking decidedly strong now, allowing for you to make a very good impression all round. This is also not a time during which you should have to do things more than once. Indeed, with a little concentration you should be making a great deal of headway.

3 WEDNESDAY
Moon Age Day 28   Moon Sign Pisces

The rewarding social interlude continues and today it might offer you the chance to get ahead in some unexpected ways. Professionally speaking, things have rarely looked better than they do at present so take advantage of these positive trends. Although a good deal of concentration is still required, your progress should be marked.

4 THURSDAY
Moon Age Day 29   Moon Sign Pisces

Although today's trends are quite progressive, tomorrow's will be less so. All the more reason to concentrate on the job at hand and to do whatever you can to make headway. At work, you could be on the winning side of a difference of opinion but it is very important that you are not seen to gloat about your success.

5 FRIDAY
Moon Age Day 0   Moon Sign Aries

As the lunar low arrives, your chart suggests that you could face something of an uphill struggle today but this will only happen if you allow it to. If at all possible, leave responsibilities and specific jobs until a slightly later date. Not everything turns out exactly as you might wish, but if you are not sailing against the wind you may hardly notice.

6 SATURDAY
Moon Age Day 1   Moon Sign Aries

You can expect this to be a routine kind of Saturday. Ring the changes socially if you can, or perhaps hand out some pleasant compliments to those who are closest to you. Stick to what you know and enjoy the company of those you love. With just a few sensible precautions, the lunar low won't have much of a bearing on your day.

7 SUNDAY
Moon Age Day 2   Moon Sign Taurus

Some positive relationship highlights continue unabated under today's trends. Avoid getting on the wrong side of your partner, because that would spoil the sort of magic that is around today. It also appears that one or two friends may be feeding you with slightly suspect information, so heed any nagging doubts in your mind.

8 MONDAY
Moon Age Day 3   Moon Sign Taurus

Today's trends favour group situations, and as you appear to identify with the aims and intentions of a group of which you are a part, this should suit you down to the ground. People should be quite willing to back you up, even when your ideas are somewhat contentious. Don't do anything to provoke jealousy between another couple.

9 TUESDAY
Moon Age Day 4   Moon Sign Gemini

Getting some peace and privacy won't be easy now but it looks as though this won't worry you. On the contrary, you should be keen to shine. In truth, the best of all worlds would involve something of a balance. Even though you enjoy the cut and thrust of life, even you are capable of becoming exhausted.

10 WEDNESDAY   *Moon Age Day 5   Moon Sign Gemini*

Today could be somewhat taxing, especially if extra demands are being made of you. Most likely these will come in the home environment. Since you still have lots of energy, it might be the evening before you collapse into a chair, but after only a few hours rest you are likely to be up and about again, such are the recuperative powers of all Air signs.

11 THURSDAY   *Moon Age Day 6   Moon Sign Gemini*

What turns out to be a rather demanding period is, nevertheless, potentially very rewarding. Your intellect is being stretched, though this fact alone is no worry to you. A cry for assistance from somewhere close by could be quite silent, but your intuition ought to ensure that you hear it, and know where it is coming from.

12 FRIDAY   *Moon Age Day 7   Moon Sign Cancer*

It is all too easy to stumble over obstacles, even if most of them are mental rather than physical. Check and recheck all facts and figures. It is very important to get things right first time and to make sure that the right sort of assistance is at hand when you need it the most. Friends should be extra kind today.

13 SATURDAY   *Moon Age Day 8   Moon Sign Cancer*

The most rewarding area of life just at present will be at home. Although the weekend offers fun and variety, you will be enjoying a good deal of it with family members or your partner. Domestic problems from the past are now likely to be sorted out and a congenial atmosphere prevails.

14 SUNDAY   *Moon Age Day 9   Moon Sign Leo*

Sunday shows little slackening of pace, though it might bring you the chance to look at certain matters in detail. There are routines to address early in the day, but later you will want to make personal contact with others. The evening especially could turn out to be very enjoyable and quite rewarding.

15 MONDAY
Moon Age Day 10   Moon Sign Leo

New romantic possibilities seem to be on the horizon and if you are single you won't want to turn them down without at least a sensible look at the possibilities. Give as good as you get in discussions, and especially so if you feel you are under unjustifiable attack. Nipping problems in the bud is definitely the way to deal with them now.

16 TUESDAY
Moon Age Day 11   Moon Sign Virgo

There may be the odd setback where social arrangements are concerned, which in itself could be somewhat irritating. On the whole however, the planets line up reasonably well for you at this stage of the working week. Don't be too quick to put brand new plans into action at work.

17 WEDNESDAY
Moon Age Day 12   Moon Sign Virgo

There could be important discussions today, but you don't want them to turn into disputes and should make that fact as clear as you can, early in the day. If you have a test or examination in front of you, now is the time to start boning up on those all important questions. Concentration counts today.

18 THURSDAY
Moon Age Day 13   Moon Sign Libra

Make an early start with important plans and once you have made your mind up to a specific course of action, don't let anything hold you back. The lunar high offers better communication skills, together with a stronger influence over others and the chance to let the world know exactly what you can do.

19 FRIDAY
Moon Age Day 14   Moon Sign Libra

A physical and mental peak is achieved, so that any tiredness that might have been around you recently now fades into the background. The day can be a whirl of activity, as well as a particularly good place to be in terms of love. Spend at least a little time thinking about people who live far away.

20 SATURDAY   *Moon Age Day 15   Moon Sign Scorpio*

The greatest fulfilment in your life right now comes from group involvements of one sort or another. Although you can easily manage on your own, it appears that things do work out better when you are willing to take on board what others think. Getting your head together with them should not be a problem.

21 SUNDAY   *Moon Age Day 16   Moon Sign Scorpio*

You tend to be attracted to unconventional types today and make it very plain that you are not prepared for a run-of-the-mill sort of Sunday. The more excitement you can pack in, the greater is the enjoyment you derive from life. In personal relationships you should not be too quick to jump to conclusions.

22 MONDAY   *Moon Age Day 17   Moon Sign Sagittarius*

Socially speaking, you can expect some positive responses from others at the moment. It financial terms, whilst you won't feel yourself to be exactly rich today, there could be slightly more money around than you had been expecting. Ideas from the past could well begin to mature any time now.

23 TUESDAY   *Moon Age Day 18   Moon Sign Sagittarius*

Social events are particularly well highlighted and remain so for the next couple of days. Getting the person you care about the most to feel special is important, particularly if they have been down for some reason. There is a very selfless feel to Libra at present, which others will love.

24 WEDNESDAY   *Moon Age Day 19   Moon Sign Capricorn*

You will probably find your peers on a similar mental wavelength to your own right now. Co-operation becomes especially important, as does your natural ability to 'share'. You might decide to stay away from subject matter that is in any way inclined to lead towards unnecessary disagreements.

25 THURSDAY · *Moon Age Day 20 · Moon Sign Capricorn*

The tendency towards being easily bored is strong, which is why it would be good to indulge in as many different activities as you can right now. It also appears that confidences are coming in from almost every direction, which could mean that you know more about the private lives of others than you do about your own!

26 FRIDAY · *Moon Age Day 21 · Moon Sign Capricorn*

Life offers its own tonic when it comes to mixing with others and it seems clear that you are in the market for excitement. Whether you can pack as much into today as you would wish remains to be seen. There are going to be moments during which it will be difficult to explain yourself fully.

27 SATURDAY · *Moon Age Day 22 · Moon Sign Aquarius*

There are some limitations around, particularly in terms of love. Maybe the one you care about the most is unwilling to share their innermost feelings with you, or it could be possible that you find yourself the subject of a jealous outburst. It might simply be easier to spend as much time today as you can with friends.

28 SUNDAY · *Moon Age Day 23 · Moon Sign Aquarius*

There can be some slight downsides to life under the present trends, and one of these may be the fact that you find it rather difficult to come to terms with the opinions of your partner. Avoid arguing about anything but do be willing to take part in reasonable discussions in which you do as much listening as talking.

29 MONDAY · *Moon Age Day 24 · Moon Sign Pisces*

What matters most of all now is that avenues of communication are wide open to you. The more you choose to get out and about, the greater will be the rewards that come your way. You may feel that it is very important to look right today and a good attitude towards presentation is genuinely of significance at this time.

30 TUESDAY

Moon Age Day 25   Moon Sign Pisces

An improvement to the smooth running of plans may be the only thing to set today apart. Although life is not exactly tedious right now, it isn't likely to be especially exciting either. Of course, there's nothing at all to prevent you from putting in that extra bit of effort that will count, so get cracking.

May

2019

1 WEDNESDAY

Moon Age Day 26   Moon Sign Pisces

Your capacity for keeping a clear head is noteworthy today and you may just discover that you can come by a bargain as a result. Certainly it would be difficult for anyone to deceive you right now and your sense of humour is also useful when you find yourself in social situations.

2 THURSDAY

Moon Age Day 27   Moon Sign Aries

Along comes a time for contemplation, rather than action. During the two days that the Moon occupies your opposite zodiac sign, it would be best to watch and wait. Avoid confusion by telling people the way you feel about situations, though as always some tact and a good helping of diplomacy would be sensible.

3 FRIDAY

Moon Age Day 28   Moon Sign Aries

Success and progress prove to be modest today, but that doesn't mean you fail to make any sort of headway at all. On the contrary, with patience, perseverance and limited expectations, the lunar low need not hamper you too much. In friendship situations, it is the people you have known the longest who are most important.

4 SATURDAY

Moon Age Day 0   Moon Sign Taurus

Personal relationships look especially promising under today's planetary trends. If you have a long-term partner there should be some extra happiness coming along, while Librans who have been looking for love really should keep their eyes open around this time. Whatever your situation, expect to enjoy some warm attention.

5 SUNDAY
Moon Age Day 1   Moon Sign Taurus

Social outings would be pleasant, so this could be a Sunday to enjoy getting out and about, especially if the early summer weather is kind. Librans who have decided to take a break at this time should be luckiest of all. And speaking of luck, you might think in terms of a small flutter now, although think this through before you gamble any small amount of money.

6 MONDAY
Moon Age Day 2   Moon Sign Taurus

Socially speaking, you are now entering a busy and quite entertaining period. Keep ahead of the work and then you will leave yourself a number of hours during which you can do more or less whatever you wish. Contributing to the successes of family members can prove to be rewarding today.

7 TUESDAY
Moon Age Day 3   Moon Sign Gemini

Beware of impulse purchases, especially for items to do with house and home. You would be far better off hanging on to your money, at least for another three or four days. Look instead for excitement in the company of people you find to be both interesting and stimulating. Love may come knocking later.

8 WEDNESDAY
Moon Age Day 4   Moon Sign Gemini

Mistakes made today could be down to unrealistic thinking on your part. This is not a state of affairs that should persist for too long, but you will need to exercise a little realism. There are plenty of things you can do right now, and only a few options that are limited. The importance today lies in knowing the difference.

9 THURSDAY
Moon Age Day 5   Moon Sign Cancer

You have what it takes now to be successful at just about anything you turn your mind to. The real reason for this, however, is that you are only undertaking things you already understand well. When viewed by others, you appear to be so full of confidence and capability as to be remarkable. Only you know your secret!

10 FRIDAY
Moon Age Day 6   Moon Sign Cancer

Emotions are close to the surface and you are more than inclined today to say exactly what you think. That's fine, but are you really only storing up trouble for yourself later on? There is nothing wrong with being truthful, but it is sometimes better not to say anything than to risk offending others.

11 SATURDAY
Moon Age Day 7   Moon Sign Leo

Close ties and emotional relationships offer the best side of life as the weekend gets started. With plenty to play for on the financial front, you might even notice a little luck coming your way. Although there is no fortune around the corner, you can still afford to back your hunches if you are sure of them.

12 SUNDAY
Moon Age Day 8   Moon Sign Leo

You need your favourite people around you today if you are going to get the most out of this Sunday. Libra is certainly not likely to be a loner right now and you are also in the mood for bright lights. Keep ahead of the game, both socially and with regard to the way you are running relationships.

13 MONDAY
Moon Age Day 9   Moon Sign Virgo

You will want to be as busy as possible today, surging into a new working week with all the energy you can muster. Don't be in the least surprised if people are picking up on your infectious sense of humour. You could be singled out for special treatment by someone you didn't even consider a friend only a short while ago.

14 TUESDAY
Moon Age Day 10   Moon Sign Virgo

Dealing with others becomes more pleasant and rewarding under today's trends. Perhaps you have been pushing yourself too hard? If so, now is the time to redress the balance by concentrating more or less completely on having fun. Even if you are using a great deal of physical energy, you can still benefit greatly.

15 WEDNESDAY   *Moon Age Day 11   Moon Sign Libra*

Now you should be really motoring. The pace of your life ought to feel busy, fast and exciting as the lunar high moves into your chart. Friends should be supportive, and they may share some good ideas with you. Socially speaking you will be on top form, and you are also well in the market for compliments.

16 THURSDAY   *Moon Age Day 12   Moon Sign Libra*

The good times continue. Lady Luck should be on your side, and this is the part of the month when you can afford to chance your arm a little. He or she who dares really does tend to win now. Of course, you need to exercise a little caution, but too much unnecessary care is for the birds now. It's dynamism and sparkle that count.

17 FRIDAY   *Moon Age Day 13   Moon Sign Scorpio*

Influences regarding personal relationships could be less favourable just now and if this were the case it would be best not to push matters too hard. You might find it is easier to concentrate on more casual associations for the time being and to leave big emotional discussions to sort out on another day.

18 SATURDAY   *Moon Age Day 14   Moon Sign Scorpio*

Your happiest times at the moment seem to be when you are in groups, where you can find a certain sort of freedom and the level of support that could be lacking in other areas of your life. Be determined in practical matters and push forward with an idea, even if not everyone agrees with you.

19 SUNDAY   *Moon Age Day 15   Moon Sign Scorpio*

A lift in most social matters is apt to bring out the best in you and it is also possible that you feel a familiar closeness in relationships that might have been missing for a while. Being on the same mental wavelength as colleagues and friends can also help to create a calmer state of mind.

20 MONDAY   *Moon Age Day 16   Moon Sign Sagittarius*

There is just a chance that you could upset the status quo today, most probably at work. This may be no bad thing, as you certainly won't want to find yourself stuck in any sort of rut. Pointless regulations will certainly get on your nerves today and you can prove awkward if unduly crossed or threatened by them.

21 TUESDAY   *Moon Age Day 17   Moon Sign Sagittarius*

A quite hectic phase comes along, and this is one that more or less demands that you keep up with all the news and views in your vicinity. A degree of success is likely to be staring you in the face, probably as a result of things you did in the past. Being certain of yourself is part of what makes today easy.

22 WEDNESDAY   *Moon Age Day 18   Moon Sign Capricorn*

Don't rely too much on the support of colleagues or even friends today because when you need it the most, it may go missing. Depend on your own judgement and, if necessary, on that of a very close friend. You are definitely inclined to keep work and play apart now, which could be a good thing.

23 THURSDAY   *Moon Age Day 19   Moon Sign Capricorn*

Domestic matters, which you sometimes find tedious beyond words, now seem warm, comfortable and even desirable. Maybe you have been expecting too much of yourself recently because this can make you nervy and inclined to run for cover. However, your love affair with the intimacies of home life could be short-lived.

24 FRIDAY   *Moon Age Day 20   Moon Sign Aquarius*

Attracting the kind thoughts and goodwill of others certainly should not be difficult for you now. There is nothing at all wrong with asking for help when you need it and especially not when those around you are so willing to offer support. You may find that you are able to break down a barrier that has been in place for months or even years.

25 SATURDAY *Moon Age Day 21   Moon Sign Aquarius*

This is a stop–start sort of day because some of what you want to do is a breeze, whilst other issues seem to be much more awkward. The general advice is to concentrate on what you can do and not to fret over things you can't. Even a single job done well makes your efforts worthwhile at the moment.

26 SUNDAY *Moon Age Day 22   Moon Sign Aquarius*

You really will just love to be yourself this Sunday, and others love you for it. Of course you can't please everyone but that's the way life is. This would be a perfect time for a change of scenery and for being in the company of people who think you are absolutely fantastic. Humility is not your special gift right now.

27 MONDAY *Moon Age Day 23   Moon Sign Pisces*

There could be something missing today and it is almost certain that you cannot put your finger on what it might be. It may not be worthwhile trying to find out because you can trust your instincts, which are well honed. By the evening you could be looking for comfort and security.

28 TUESDAY *Moon Age Day 24   Moon Sign Pisces*

Social plans may have to be re-routed but since you are very good at thinking on your feet, this is not likely to be too much of a problem. A planned schedule is less likely to get you where you want to be than one that involves reacting to events. Romantically speaking, you could be entering a very interesting phase.

29 WEDNESDAY *Moon Age Day 25   Moon Sign Aries*

Don't take on too many commitments today. The lunar low has come around and is almost certain to sap your strength. Concentrate on things you enjoy and, if possible, take a total break from responsibilities. You can't expect everyone to agree with your ideas for today or tomorrow so be patient.

30 THURSDAY *Moon Age Day 26   Moon Sign Aries*

The pace of life isn't running at fever pitch, in fact you can afford to amble along for once. Get what you can from relationships at home or amongst really good friends. The quieter your pastimes are at the moment, the happier you will probably be. Libra is not generally a solitary sign but is inclined to be so at present.

31 FRIDAY *Moon Age Day 27   Moon Sign Aries*

You should be able to attract life's little luxuries today, something that doesn't generally cross your mind unless you are feeling insecure. It ought to be obvious that your instincts are presently honed to perfection and with a mixture of intuition and direct communication, understanding communication with others ought to be straightforward.

June

2019

1 SATURDAY
Moon Age Day 28   Moon Sign Taurus

This could be a fairly intriguing sort of day and one on which information gathering is the best part of it. Your curiosity is likely to be aroused from the moment you get up. Anything that is particularly odd or unusual could catch your attention and this might prove to be an ideal time for shopping, particularly for antiques.

2 SUNDAY
Moon Age Day 29   Moon Sign Taurus

Current trends suggest that you can make the best of what is happening around you, particularly in terms of finances. If you have to sign any contracts or documents, this is a period during which you are willing to take the time to read the small print. This fact alone may prove to be extremely fortuitous later.

3 MONDAY
Moon Age Day 0   Moon Sign Gemini

You should be on top form in get-togethers with both relatives and friends at the moment. You are also very shrewd and someone would have to get up very early in the day to get one over on you. Keep yourself tuned in to the needs of your partner, and offer support to a friend if they are having problems.

4 TUESDAY
Moon Age Day 1   Moon Sign Gemini

Now is a time you may choose to seek out a little peace and quiet, away from the cut and thrust that has been so much a part of your life for the last few days. What you won't have failed to notice is that the weather is improving. A little fresh air and some congenial company are called for, although you may not feel like going anywhere boisterous.

5 WEDNESDAY   *Moon Age Day 2   Moon Sign Cancer*

Don't be in too much of a hurry to get practical jobs out of the way as your chart suggests that at least some of them would be better off left until later. It is the abstract that suits you best now, together with a tremendous impulse to travel. Staying in the same place for long at a time really goes against the grain under present astrological trends.

6 THURSDAY   *Moon Age Day 3   Moon Sign Cancer*

A plan of action out there in the competitive world is definitely called for. Be aware of the fact that not everyone is likely to be on your side today. A quality that has been shining out noticeably over the last few weeks is intuition. Today is no different with that regard, so listen to your inner thoughts and their advice.

7 FRIDAY   *Moon Age Day 4   Moon Sign Leo*

Though financial and material plans are likely to be on course, not everyone who surrounds you today is as happy as you are. If at all possible, remove yourself from people who are in a negative mood so that you can be around joyful people, whose attitudes reflect your own. If you feel insecure at any stage there should be someone you can talk to.

8 SATURDAY   *Moon Age Day 5   Moon Sign Leo*

Getting along with others is not at all hard for Libra now, so this could turn out to be an ideal weekend for mixing with friends and family. Certainly, you will not want to spend all that much time on your own, and you will crave the company of people who make you laugh and who have something interesting to say.

9 SUNDAY   *Moon Age Day 6   Moon Sign Virgo*

The go-getting side of your nature is especially apparent now. There is very little that is likely to hold you back, once you have made up your mind to a particular course of action. Nevertheless, you remain good to know and should certainly want to find time to please family members and friends alike.

10 MONDAY
Moon Age Day 7   Moon Sign Virgo

Present planetary influences keep you happily on the go and yet another working week commences with a great deal of action on your part. If you are between jobs, or perhaps retired, you won't have any difficulty filling your time. On the contrary, most of the useful hours of the day pass in a blur.

11 TUESDAY
Moon Age Day 8   Moon Sign Virgo

Emotional issues are likely to be on your mind at the present time. Don't be too quick to take a decision based upon them that you may come to regret at a later stage. Where a particular task you don't care for is concerned, get it out of the way as soon as you can today. The contemplation of it is worse than its fulfilment.

12 WEDNESDAY
Moon Age Day 9   Moon Sign Libra

The green light is definitely on now and you will be doing anything you can to be the centre of attention. Bright lights and exciting times are what appeal the most, together with a tremendous love of life in general. There are gains to be made, not least of all because your luck is in at the moment.

13 THURSDAY
Moon Age Day 10   Moon Sign Libra

Positive spirits are still in great supply, together with the good times that accompany them. This might turn out to be a favourable time for making financial gains, partly through investment but also on account of your intuition. Something very surprising could come your way, either materially or in terms of remarks.

14 FRIDAY
Moon Age Day 11   Moon Sign Scorpio

It is probable that you think you are right about a host of things at present. This may well be the case but you won't help your cause if you force the situation home too much. A little humility goes a long way, particularly when there are people around who could be of great practical use to you.

15 SATURDAY   *Moon Age Day 12   Moon Sign Scorpio*

This is a time when you notice that financial issues come into better focus. You can afford to back your hunches, though you would be unlikely to be parting with much money. What you are best at right now is planning for later – often a strong point for anyone born under the sign of the Scales.

16 SUNDAY   *Moon Age Day 13   Moon Sign Sagittarius*

Right now you are mainly concerned with practical ideas, so the theoretical side of life is taking something of a back seat. That's fine but it could be that you discover yourself doing the same thing more than once, simply because you haven't thought it through first. A few minutes contemplation can save hours now.

17 MONDAY   *Moon Age Day 14   Moon Sign Sagittarius*

Another day where financial gain looks possible, especially if you handle things properly. You should find you can get plenty done in a practical sense and you are now less likely to have to repeat yourself. There are strong incentives coming along to make significant changes in and around your home but you are going to need help.

18 TUESDAY   *Moon Age Day 15   Moon Sign Capricorn*

There is no reason to hang back at this stage of this week and it is important that you take opportunities as and when they arise. Having said that, you may feel slightly more impatient than you did yesterday, and if this were the case it would be sensible to listen to what someone else has to say before you rush into something that you later regret.

19 WEDNESDAY   *Moon Age Day 16   Moon Sign Capricorn*

Look out for romantic opportunities – that is if they don't find you first. Choosing the right words to say, in order to make the best of impressions should be child's play at the moment and you revel in the affection that comes your way. This really is a magical period in your life and almost all Libran's should realise it to be so.

20 THURSDAY — *Moon Age Day 17   Moon Sign Capricorn*

Now is a time when you should discover that you don't have to push too hard to make financial progress. It may come to you a result of the actions of others so be very sure to offer sincere thanks when they come due. Away from monetary matters, take time out to show someone just how very special they are to you.

21 FRIDAY — *Moon Age Day 18   Moon Sign Aquarius*

Your temporarily strong opinions will not appeal to everyone today and as a result you could be somewhat argumentative. This won't really do you any good and it would be more sensible to remain quiet, especially when you know that you are on shaky ground. A few solitary hours would do you no harm right now.

22 SATURDAY — *Moon Age Day 19   Moon Sign Aquarius*

It's time to look at your personal economy and to take decisions into your own hands. Not everyone will agree but you have good powers of communication at present and should not find it difficult to bring others round. There are gains and losses this weekend but on balance you should prove to be the winner.

23 SUNDAY — *Moon Age Day 20   Moon Sign Pisces*

You should now try to consolidate what you have started personally and not allow technicalities to get in your way. Libra shows it is very determined at present but also has generosity of spirit on a scale that will surprise even you. Although you can't have everything you want today, much you desire may come your way.

24 MONDAY — *Moon Age Day 21   Moon Sign Pisces*

You should now be pressing ahead diligently with professional incentives as trends assist Libra to work harder at this stage than at any other time during June. This means you will get plenty done and that you should be quite happy with your progress by the time the evening comes along. Then it's time to have some fun.

111

25 TUESDAY   *Moon Age Day 22   Moon Sign Pisces*

You may need to be very aware of whom you are willing to trust right now. Friends you have known for a long time are probably fine but there could be one or two people about who do intend to mislead you in some way. Your intuition is strong and should be your best guide at present.

26 WEDNESDAY   *Moon Age Day 23   Moon Sign Aries*

A few unexpected financial hiccups are possible around now. Give yourself a pat on the back for solving them quickly but don't take your eye off the ball as far as longer-term fiscal arrangements are concerned. You might be planning a journey either now or soon, which could prove to be quite exciting.

27 THURSDAY   *Moon Age Day 24   Moon Sign Aries*

It is true that the lunar low can slow you down, though almost certainly not for long. Ingenious as you are, you will find ways around problems and give yourself a head start for the most positive trends that stand just around the corner. A friend could be offering you some sensible and timely advice.

28 FRIDAY   *Moon Age Day 25   Moon Sign Taurus*

The control you once felt confident that you had over life may now feel somewhat diminished, so prepare for this to not be the best day in living memory. However, a personal issue may prove encouraging so it is therefore probably the personal side of life that offers the best opportunities for gain right now.

29 SATURDAY   *Moon Age Day 26   Moon Sign Taurus*

This should be a generally light-hearted sort of day and not a period during which you will be taking yourself or anyone else very seriously. You constantly look for new ways to put your versatile powers to the test and may set out to overturn some of the obstacles life has placed in your path before.

30 SUNDAY
Moon Age Day 27   Moon Sign Gemini

Curiosity and your intellectual abilities are well marked in your chart today. Any sort of mystery is certain to grab your imagination and you won't be in the least tardy when it comes to turning over a few stones. Family members should prove to be very supportive and will offer you new possibilities to think about at home.

July

2019

1 MONDAY
Moon Age Day 28   Moon Sign Gemini

You should now be in a good position to call the shots regarding future plans, especially in the workplace. Moves made today could prove to be advantageous later on and it is clear that you are filled with energy and determination. Social trends also look good, particularly for single Librans or those looking for love.

2 TUESDAY
Moon Age Day 0   Moon Sign Gemini

Your love life could turn out rather better than you had expected at this time. With plenty to go at in terms of social possibilities, and maybe fewer practical responsibilities weighing you down, it looks as though you will be doing what you can to have a good time once work is out of the way.

3 WEDNESDAY
Moon Age Day 1   Moon Sign Cancer

Whilst present trends are helpful in a financial sense, there might be some awkward people about. This combined with the fact that you may need to come to terms with an issue that has been on your mind for a while may lead to some challenges today. Don't get carried away with little details, as it is the overview of matters that counts the most.

4 THURSDAY
Moon Age Day 2   Moon Sign Cancer

Coming to a decision regarding an important personal matter might mean the end of a particular phase now. This doesn't necessarily have to be a bad thing at all. On the contrary, you are quite committed to the future and, as usual, trying to get a thousand different things done all at the same time.

5 FRIDAY   *Moon Age Day 3   Moon Sign Leo*

Everyday interactions can bring enlightening experiences now. This is a day during which you will want to keep your eyes wide open because there are opportunities coming your way. If you want to enjoy yourself in the weekend that lies ahead, it may be necessary to put some extra effort in now.

6 SATURDAY   *Moon Age Day 4   Moon Sign Leo*

Matters of the heart now have a lot going for them, so much so that a good deal of your thinking time is taken up in that direction. Creative possibilities are a big part of the deal that is on offer today and it could be that you are considering quite extensive changes around house and home.

7 SUNDAY   *Moon Age Day 5   Moon Sign Virgo*

You should enjoy some ongoing success where monetary matters are concerned. Although Sunday may not turn out to be particularly startling itself, the plans you lay down now should see you somewhat better off before long. Your confidence to say the right thing in public situations is certainly not lacking.

8 MONDAY   ☿   *Moon Age Day 6   Moon Sign Virgo*

The new week brings big ideas, but are you really in a position to make the most of them? Active as ever, but perhaps inclined to rush into things a little, you will need a certain amount of circumspection if you are going to get the best out of the day. An impromptu journey could prove to be very interesting.

9 TUESDAY   ☿   *Moon Age Day 7   Moon Sign Libra*

Along comes the lunar high, adding even more impetus to what is already a generally positive phase in any case. Your expectations of life are high, but there is little reason to suggest that you will be let down in any way. Better-than-average luck means that you can probably afford to speculate a little, so perhaps a day at the races is in order!

10 WEDNESDAY ☿   *Moon Age Day 8*   *Moon Sign Libra*

From somewhere or other you drum up the energy to keep up the pace and make the most of another potentially successful day. So much is going your way astrologically right now that you should be spoilt for choice. Keep talking and make certain that the people who count the most are listening carefully.

11 THURSDAY ☿   *Moon Age Day 9*   *Moon Sign Scorpio*

Much of what is really rewarding in your life at present centres around home and family. Although you are keeping busy, it is towards your domain that your thoughts are inclined to stray for now. Why not arrange a social gathering at home, so that you can share the place you cherish the most with your friends?

12 FRIDAY ☿   *Moon Age Day 10*   *Moon Sign Scorpio*

Do you get the feeling there is something you have forgotten? Think carefully, because trends suggest that you will struggle to avoid getting at least some things wrong around now. Your creative potential is strong, and you may feel inclined to direct this towards alterations in your home or garden. This is likely to be a very active day, and probably a very happy one.

13 SATURDAY ☿ *Moon Age Day 11* *Moon Sign Sagittarius*

Your judgement appears to be sound and you show an attractive face to the world at large. If not everyone wishes to be your friend – well, there are plenty of people who do. Stay away from a minor dispute in the family that might turn out to be much more in the fullness of time.

14 SUNDAY ☿ *Moon Age Day 12* *Moon Sign Sagittarius*

Though obligations to others can prove to be somewhat tiresome today, in the main you are jogging through life quite merrily. Arrangements for travel could be on your mind and some lucky Librans will be going off on holiday around now. Make the most of new enterprises that offer financial incentives.

15 MONDAY   ☿ *Moon Age Day 13*   *Moon Sign Capricorn*

Money-wise you ought to find that things are coming together quite nicely at this time. If there are congratulations to be made, to a family member or friend, make a big deal of the situation. Be careful what you ask others to do for you today because a refusal on their part could prove quite annoying.

16 TUESDAY   ☿ *Moon Age Day 14*   *Moon Sign Capricorn*

Your financial wherewithal is likely to be better and it might be possible for you to make some fairly straightforward speculations because your mind is working very clearly now. Friends show how important you are and this definitely feeds your ego. You may be called upon to lend someone a hand, particularly by relatives.

17 WEDNESDAY ☿ *Moon Age Day 15*   *Moon Sign Capricorn*

You can expect a few ups and downs today, most likely in terms of relationships. Although you have what it takes to get on the right side of most people, there are always going to be exceptions. Expect rules and regulations to get on your nerves, but accept the fact that all you can do is shrug your shoulders and smile.

18 THURSDAY   ☿ *Moon Age Day 16*   *Moon Sign Aquarius*

You should be on the move today and happy to have things going your way. There isn't much mileage in staying in the same place and travel of any sort is supported by a number of present trends. In sporting activities you will be going for gold, though it has to be said that you might only manage silver.

19 FRIDAY   ☿ *Moon Age Day 17*   *Moon Sign Aquarius*

You find the activities that are taking place out there in the wider world more appealing than home-based matters today. That's fine, as long as you don't appear to be deliberately ignoring your nearest and dearest. Libra is for now a creature of the moment and should realise it, but some consideration is still necessary.

20 SATURDAY ☿ *Moon Age Day 18 Moon Sign Pisces*

Casual conversations might not seem to get you anywhere as a rule but they can today. Keep your ears open because the truth of many situations lies just below the surface. Routines can be something of a bind and don't leave you the amount of time you feel you need to get on with those important details.

21 SUNDAY ☿ *Moon Age Day 19 Moon Sign Pisces*

Impatience can clearly be a factor this Sunday and is something you will most probably wish to avoid. Getting on the wrong side of a relative won't do you any good at all and this could mean having to bite your tongue. It might annoy you now but you will be glad you did it in the fullness of time.

22 MONDAY ☿ *Moon Age Day 20 Moon Sign Pisces*

You could encounter a few obstacles at the moment so don't be too quick to take the initiative if the way ahead seems clear to you. Don't allow your own sense of your limitations to hold you back – many of them are just transitory. Concerted effort counts later but for now you can afford to be just a little circumspect.

23 TUESDAY ☿ *Moon Age Day 21 Moon Sign Aries*

Delays on the road to some of your goals are unavoidable at the moment. It might seem as if life has put the brakes on, but what is really happening is that you are looking more carefully at certain situations. Not every delay is necessarily a bad thing, and at least you have time for some rest and recuperation.

24 WEDNESDAY ☿ *Moon Age Day 22 Moon Sign Aries*

The lunar low continues and there isn't that much you can do about it. Better by far to show a realistic face to the world and to enjoy the quieter aspects of life that are yours for the taking at the moment. A great deal is still going your way; it's simply that you may not appreciate it at present.

25 THURSDAY ☿ *Moon Age Day 23 Moon Sign Taurus*

In terms of your relationships with others, what seemed so easy a few days ago is certainly looking more difficult now. You may be unwilling to compromise and this fact alone can get you into some hot water. Arriving at conclusions that don't really make sense is also another potential difficulty. Bear these trends in mind and take stock of your own behaviour.

26 FRIDAY ☿ *Moon Age Day 24 Moon Sign Taurus*

Though this may prove to be a rather taxing phase as far as work is concerned, in a general sense things should still be going the way you would wish. You won't take kindly to being told what to do, but compromise is important and you are clearly bright enough to allow others to believe they are getting their own way even if you are managing things behind the scenes.

27 SATURDAY ☿ *Moon Age Day 25 Moon Sign Taurus*

Be on the lookout for old faces coming once again into your life. The present position of the Moon makes it likely that meetings with those from the past can have some sort of positive bearing on your immediate future. There is much about today that could be seen as odd or unusual but this is no bad thing.

28 SUNDAY ☿ *Moon Age Day 26 Moon Sign Gemini*

The art of good conversation, together with the attendant popularity that comes your way as a result, is definitely your forte at present. However, not everything you hear at the moment is of equal importance and it is vitally important that you take time to sort out the wheat from the chaff.

29 MONDAY ☿ *Moon Age Day 27 Moon Sign Gemini*

As far as personal and emotional security is concerned, you should find yourself very well looked after today. For the first time in days there appear to be moments to sit and take stock and you won't be in too much of a rush to get things done. Something that has been a problem could even solve itself today.

30 TUESDAY ☿ *Moon Age Day 28 Moon Sign Cancer*

You are certainly not backward at coming forward, which is going to stand you in good stead at work. Whether all you have to say is of interest to everyone you meet might be somewhat in doubt and it is important to know when you are over-egging the pudding. Balance is required.

31 WEDNESDAY ☿ *Moon Age Day 0 Moon Sign Cancer*

As the planets move on, the circumstances become more favourable for dealing with money matters. You have a good head on your shoulders during the middle of this week and seem likely to be making an impression on those who have power and influence. In your personal life, though, you might encounter some awkward types.

August 2019

1 THURSDAY
Moon Age Day 1   Moon Sign Leo

Matters should be falling quite nicely into place around the beginning of this month. This is especially true in a career sense but also with regard to personal relationships. You seem to be fairly organised at present and to have a good idea of how others are likely to react under any given set of circumstances.

2 FRIDAY
Moon Age Day 2   Moon Sign Leo

Socially speaking this ought to be a fairly positive sort of day. Routines may be something of a drag, but if you choose not to let them override you but slot them in around other tasks this might not turn out to be the case. Don't be worried about asking for assistance, too. There are people around you who are only too willing to help.

3 SATURDAY
Moon Age Day 3   Moon Sign Virgo

Your influence concerning everyday matters is somewhat limited at this time and might not be helped by the fact that the information you receive is not entirely reliable. If you are faced with a rather awe-inspiring task, the best course of action is to break it down into manageable units.

4 SUNDAY
Moon Age Day 4   Moon Sign Virgo

This is a day when it would be sensible not to get on the wrong side of people in authority. You may feel unafraid to stick up for yourself and others – sometimes in a reckless manner – which is most untypical of Libra. Think before you speak and don't take a specific stance you know is certain to annoy someone who has a hold over you.

5 MONDAY
Moon Age Day 5   Moon Sign Libra

Fortune has a part to play in your endeavours today. Even when you think you are not making the right moves, circumstances should alter to suit you. Although you may not consider yourself to be a particularly lucky person, what happens during today and for a few days to come could prove you wrong.

6 TUESDAY
Moon Age Day 6   Moon Sign Libra

Put your impressive personality to the test and show the world what you are capable of. There is massive support around when you are willing to go out and look for it, not to mention that you have more than your fair share of talent. Libra shines, and this is something everyone is quite keen to see.

7 WEDNESDAY
Moon Age Day 7   Moon Sign Scorpio

Everyday matters could become slightly more interesting today. Some potentially positive encounters with others are indicated, giving you the opportunity to shine, particularly in an intellectual sense. Showing the world how bright you are helps to feed your ego, which isn't half as strong and resilient as people think it is.

8 THURSDAY
Moon Age Day 8   Moon Sign Scorpio

There is much to be gained now from simple talks and discussion at any level, but particularly in a domestic sense. Useful information comes your way from a host of different directions, so that success is partly a matter of keeping your ears open. Be careful how you approach someone who is usually prickly.

9 FRIDAY
Moon Age Day 9   Moon Sign Sagittarius

The focus now tends to be upon leisure and your social life, which is not at all surprising at this time of year. Make sure that you get some time out of doors. All the hard work in the world is only sensible if you know how to enjoy yourself when you are not toiling away. Allow someone else to take the strain for a little while.

10 SATURDAY *Moon Age Day 10   Moon Sign Sagittarius*

There appears to be little reason why you cannot get ahead this weekend, though this is much more likely in a social, rather than a professional sense. There are people in your vicinity who know how to have fun and you will wish to be one of them. There is nothing very serious about today, and that's the way it should be now.

11 SUNDAY *Moon Age Day 11   Moon Sign Sagittarius*

Close emotional involvement ought to prove most rewarding and interesting area of your life today. Some confusion over details regarding affairs of the heart can be resolved with just a little patience on your part. In fact, this is a day for talking and for getting on-side with people who could have been difficult to deal with previously.

12 MONDAY *Moon Age Day 12   Moon Sign Capricorn*

Though your domestic life is, on the whole, rather settled at present, there could be a slight upheaval at some stage today. Try to avoid allowing this to upset your equilibrium and settle for a steady and generally happy day. The urge to travel is strong at the moment but journeys may have to be temporarily delayed.

13 TUESDAY *Moon Age Day 13   Moon Sign Capricorn*

The atmosphere at home should be harmonious and enjoyable. Family members give you good reason to be proud of them and it may be your nearest and dearest you choose to take with you on some sort of excursion. Avoid negative people, especially in sporting contexts or where some sort of competitive edge is concerned.

14 WEDNESDAY *Moon Age Day 14   Moon Sign Aquarius*

Today's influences should have a positive bearing on all aspects of communication. Talks and discussions can work out to your advantage and bring you closer to realising a few ambitions. Love is uppermost in your mind and you could be choosing this time to show someone special how much you care.

15 THURSDAY   *Moon Age Day 15   Moon Sign Aquarius*

This would be an excellent time for getting others round to your way of thinking. Those who contribute to your life are especially sensitive to both your needs and considered thoughts at present. For this reason alone, you might choose to broach a subject you have been avoiding previously. Loving relationships should be warm.

16 FRIDAY   *Moon Age Day 16   Moon Sign Aquarius*

You might now choose to build on promising starts as far as your plans are concerned and you are looking around for the sort of support that could prove to be invaluable. Meanwhile, you should be discovering that romance is a key point of the day, with some unexpected compliments about to arrive.

17 SATURDAY   *Moon Age Day 17   Moon Sign Pisces*

Although you will clearly be trying to do a dozen different things at once right now, in the end you might have to settle for two or three. You may be versatile but you are not superhuman so bear in mind that less done well is better than more done badly. This is self-evident, though not always to you.

18 SUNDAY   *Moon Age Day 18   Moon Sign Pisces*

A period of domestic reward greets you on this Sunday. Although you might have thought that this would be a good time to be on the move, in the end what hearth and home have to offer could be better. Leave a few jobs until later, or else look around for someone else to do them for you.

19 MONDAY   *Moon Age Day 19   Moon Sign Aries*

As the lunar low arrives you will probably be lacking a little of the vitality that has come to be second nature during the last couple of weeks. At least this means you will slow down for a day or two. This is an important process because it allows you to take stock and to plan for the future.

20 TUESDAY   *Moon Age Day 20   Moon Sign Aries*

Although you could be rather less enthusiastic than you would wish to be, this fact offers others the chance to have a go. Over the last few weeks, you may have developed an attitude that believed unless you were doing things yourself, they were not being done properly. You could find out today that this is not true.

21 WEDNESDAY   *Moon Age Day 21   Moon Sign Aries*

Beware because you might not have quite the level of patience you would wish and this is especially true when you are dealing with younger people or individuals who never seem able to do the right thing. Keep a record of your achievements at present, so that you can look at them when times are less good.

22 THURSDAY   *Moon Age Day 22   Moon Sign Taurus*

You can get a great deal from your domestic circumstances and surroundings at this stage of the month, even though you might not have as much time as you would wish to spend with your family. In all probability, this is a time for travel and perhaps for holidays for a great many Librans.

23 FRIDAY   *Moon Age Day 23   Moon Sign Taurus*

Whatever you are doing today, it goes better with a helping hand. Co-operation is the key word, particularly so when you are working alongside your friends. A carefree streak is likely to run through you today, but you need to be prepared to take things more cautiously as the evening arrives.

24 SATURDAY   *Moon Age Day 24   Moon Sign Gemini*

There could be a few disappointments today, although nothing of any real consequence. You would be best advised to stick to simple things and avoid any unnecessary complications. Perhaps seek out friends you don't see very often, or alternatively spend some time with family members at home.

25 SUNDAY   *Moon Age Day 25   Moon Sign Gemini*

There is likely to be some new and important information at your disposal, probably coming from the direction of a friend or associate. It is worth paying attention today and you would be well advised to act on situations as soon as possible. Good romantic prospects seem to be in the offing.

26 MONDAY   *Moon Age Day 26   Moon Sign Cancer*

There is scope for broadening your personal horizons around now and a good deal of excitement is possible under present trends. Although you are inclined to act on impulse at the moment, your Libran know-how allows you to get away with things that others could only dream about.

27 TUESDAY   *Moon Age Day 27   Moon Sign Cancer*

In a social sense it is clear that you want to branch out at this stage of the week. Those of you who have been paying attention might have noticed that professional trends are not so obvious right now. For this reason alone, you could be in a period during which a holiday would be the very best thing.

28 WEDNESDAY   *Moon Age Day 28   Moon Sign Leo*

You benefit most today from those associations closest to home. As you enter a temporary but important thoughtful phase, the degree of success you register out there in the wider world is not so great, whereas you feel secure, happy and content when in your own abode. Listen out for an important telephone call later.

29 THURSDAY   *Moon Age Day 29   Moon Sign Leo*

You will be concentrating on whatever you think you do best today, which is probably a sensible response to present trends. What might not be so sensible would be to start too many new projects. Remember that there are only so many hours in a day and the number doesn't increase just because you are an Air-sign person.

30 FRIDAY
Moon Age Day 0   Moon Sign Virgo

The pull of the past can be especially strong around this time. Perhaps as a result of telephone calls or letters, you are drawn mentally into situations that you thought were long gone. Make sure to be positive about the present too and don't allow yourself to get too drawn into a nostalgic frame of mind.

31 SATURDAY
Moon Age Day 1   Moon Sign Virgo

If there are a great many mundane issues to deal with today, you could run out of patience. The fact is that you want to be footloose and fancy free, something that is second nature to you at present. Your confidence is gradually growing to the point where you may feel able to say something you have been thinking about for ages.

September 2019

1 SUNDAY
Moon Age Day 2   Moon Sign Libra

A major decision could be called for today and with slightly relaxed trends around you should have the time to think about it. You can spot new opportunities a mile off and although Sunday might not be the best day to put the most practical of them into action, your ability to plan is second to none.

2 MONDAY
Moon Age Day 3   Moon Sign Libra

You need to know where you are from a financial point of few and may have to firm up some decisions you have been making of late. If cash is somewhat short, turn your fertile mind to finding new ways of getting more revenue coming in. For some Librans, even a new job won't be out of the question.

3 TUESDAY
Moon Age Day 4   Moon Sign Scorpio

This is a good time for informed discussions of almost any sort. You may also decide around now to take certain aspects of your life in hand. Some Librans will be embarking on a health kick. That's fine, but if you are one of them do remember that Rome wasn't built in a day.

4 WEDNESDAY
Moon Age Day 5   Moon Sign Scorpio

You should really enjoy the sort of company you are keeping now. This can be a highly social day, filled with promise and replete with compliments that are coming in your direction. If not everyone seems to be on your side, you might spend at least part of the day discovering why, and then putting matters right.

5 THURSDAY
Moon Age Day 6   Moon Sign Scorpio

Domestic matters and issues from the past are very much on your mind at the moment. Familiar faces and much-loved places are also important. There may not be anything remarkable about today but your hours should be fairly happy and there are the sort of social contacts around that you enjoy.

6 FRIDAY
Moon Age Day 7   Moon Sign Sagittarius

A few challenges at work could see this part of the week ending on a slightly less favourable note than seemed to be the case earlier in the week. It isn't as if anything major is going wrong, merely that the way you look at situations is different from others. A really good idea that comes along later in the day should not be ignored.

7 SATURDAY
Moon Age Day 8   Moon Sign Sagittarius

There are goals and objectives that you have in mind, but whether or not you are in the market to go and get them remains to be seen. Don't take on any project in which you are beaten before you start. For this reason alone it might be better to stick with what you know for today and leave innovation until later.

8 SUNDAY
Moon Age Day 9   Moon Sign Capricorn

It's time to take centre stage and to allow that Air-sign genius to show. After a few days when you were really not shining too bright, the sun comes out again. Now you can tackle almost anything with a great sense of fun. Almost anyone you meet will show how pleased they are to know you.

9 MONDAY
Moon Age Day 10   Moon Sign Capricorn

The domestic scene should now provide all the pleasure you need in your life. People are fun to be with and there are very few individuals who will try to throw a spanner in the works of any of your ideas. More than one planet is now well placed to give you the edge, which you will not fail to use.

10 TUESDAY   *Moon Age Day 11*   *Moon Sign Aquarius*

You are not quite so easy to approach today, being naturally touchier than has been the case recently. Good friends will understand that we cannot always be on form and should make allowances for you. In professional relationships, things are different, and a good degree of deliberate tact on your part will be called for.

11 WEDNESDAY   *Moon Age Day 12*   *Moon Sign Aquarius*

This is a time when you tend to retreat, momentarily, from the world. It won't be a phase that stays around long and you are not likely to be sulking about anything. You simply have a need to think things through. Make your feelings known to people who might think they have upset you in some way and offer reassurance.

12 THURSDAY   *Moon Age Day 13*   *Moon Sign Aquarius*

Don't allow practical situations to run into the buffers simply on account of a lack of attention on your part. This is a day to watch closely what is going on and not to allow complications to arise, when you could so easily sort them out almost immediately. Leave a little time free today in which to simply enjoy yourself.

13 FRIDAY   *Moon Age Day 14*   *Moon Sign Pisces*

Along comes a period of generally high enthusiasm, together with an optimism that might not be entirely justified by circumstances. You have a tendency to dominate in romantic situations, though this could not be called a fault and is likely to work out well for you in the end.

14 SATURDAY   *Moon Age Day 15*   *Moon Sign Pisces*

There are a few illusions around today, the problem being that some of them look quite seductive. You need to be a good analyst and to avoid taking anything at face value. You don't lack confidence, but too much of that commodity can be quite destructive. Playing devil's advocate isn't fun but can be necessary.

15 SUNDAY
Moon Age Day 16   Moon Sign Aries

Trends continue in a very similar vein as yesterday. Make sure that you think things through carefully and check exactly what you are doing or signing up to before you act. Don't allow your natural confidence and faith in yourself and others to lead you somewhere you don't want to go.

16 MONDAY
Moon Age Day 17   Moon Sign Aries

Energy and enthusiasm may be in short supply as a new working week gets started. The lunar low was present yesterday and still sits upon you. As long as you realise this is an interlude, all is well. The problem is that Libra is presently a creature of the moment and tends to think that 'now' is forever.

17 TUESDAY
Moon Age Day 18   Moon Sign Aries

Love and romance are important issues for you at this stage of the week. Make sure that there is not something practical which you have forgotten and check details carefully at all stages during today. Routines you usually find boring may now offer a sense of continuity and even satisfaction.

18 WEDNESDAY
Moon Age Day 19   Moon Sign Taurus

Family developments can bring some reward though in the main you are mixing with friends and even making a few new ones. The advancing year could find you wondering about some plan or other that seems to have fallen by the wayside. Think about starting a real adventure quite soon.

19 THURSDAY
Moon Age Day 20   Moon Sign Taurus

Romance is in the air and there are plenty of opportunities to let someone know how you feel. This would be a good day for shopping and for hunting out that special bargain that has eluded you for some time. Good luck is on your side and should continue to be so into the weekend.

20 FRIDAY
Moon Age Day 21   Moon Sign Gemini

In terms of work, better results appear to be on the way. You should be co-operating well with others and you should find yourself in a reasonable position to move forward on plans that have been waiting for a while. The attitude of certain friends may be difficult to understand but keep plugging away all the same.

21 SATURDAY
Moon Age Day 22   Moon Sign Gemini

This is not a day to be dissuaded from something about which you are certain. Although you are often working on hunches at the moment, you are also very anxious to make sure your freedoms are preserved. You need to trust yourself and to convince others that you know what you are talking about.

22 SUNDAY
Moon Age Day 23   Moon Sign Gemini

Practical matters proceed more smoothly than was the case yesterday and you should at last find yourself making the kind of progress you have been looking for. There won't be much time to deal with mundane matters but you probably don't mind this too much. All the same, it's important to think things through.

23 MONDAY
Moon Age Day 24   Moon Sign Cancer

Socially speaking, this is going to be a good day, or at least it will be if you get up and about and make the most of it. The earlier you get going, the greater are the gains that are going to come your way. The path to romance is now as smooth as it is likely to be this month and present trends could lead to some interesting events.

24 TUESDAY
Moon Age Day 25   Moon Sign Cancer

There is plenty to be done today and the only real problem seems to be having to spread yourself too thinly, at least during the working day. Social trends look particularly good and you should be able to meet most of your commitments in the eyes of others. Keep up your efforts to get ahead in the financial stakes.

25 WEDNESDAY   *Moon Age Day 26   Moon Sign Leo*

Socially speaking, it is clear that you are now on a real winning streak. This is the time of the month to decide what you want and then to go out and get it. Friends may be quite demanding but that won't be a problem to a person who seems able to fit in any amount of demands and still have moments to spare.

26 THURSDAY   *Moon Age Day 27   Moon Sign Leo*

New friendships now become much more likely and some of these could easily be allied to your working circumstances. Although there are slight setbacks to be encountered at the moment, it is unlikely that any of these will stop you in your tracks. You should be as zippy and happy as ever today.

27 FRIDAY   *Moon Age Day 28   Moon Sign Virgo*

Don't get carried away with ideas that are basically impractical. Things work much better for you at present if you stick to what you know, even though for you this can seem tedious or boring. On the romantic front, you should be able to find the right words to make almost anyone fall for you in a big way.

28 SATURDAY   *Moon Age Day 0   Moon Sign Virgo*

A nostalgic mood sweeps in and has a strong bearing over the way you look at and handle events today. Perhaps you are forced by circumstances to be in the company of people you have known for a long time? Or perhaps you are being sought out for advice? Ring the changes at some stage and lighten things up.

29 SUNDAY   *Moon Age Day 1   Moon Sign Libra*

Put your best foot forward Libra, and make the most of present planetary trends. The lunar high helps to support you through new endeavours and with enterprises that need that extra bit of zip. Confident and certain of your steps, this is a time to move forward, even if you might occasionally be nervous.

30 MONDAY
Moon Age Day 2   Moon Sign Libra

You should be looking and feeling at your best around now. There are strong supporting influences, some of which work especially well in terms of romantic proposals, either made or received. Few people will question your motives or your actions today, which means you could get away with almost anything.

October
2019

1 TUESDAY
Moon Age Day 3   Moon Sign Scorpio

Personal and domestic issues come under the spotlight now. Not everyone is behaving in quite the way you might have expected and you are going to have to allow a certain degree of latitude. Another important factor about today is that you shouldn't overwork because you will tire easily at present.

2 WEDNESDAY
Moon Age Day 4   Moon Sign Scorpio

Confidence isn't exactly brimming over today but that does not have to prevent you from making a good deal of progress in minor issues. Long-term planning can be thwarted by the contrary opinions of family members and some extra latitude might be necessary if you end up dealing with people who feel they have an axe to grind.

3 THURSDAY
Moon Age Day 5   Moon Sign Sagittarius

This is a period that offers potential for relaxation and even some laziness. If this sounds odd, do bear in mind that you are almost always on the go through every waking hour. Everyone needs a break sometimes, and even you are no exception. Enjoy doing nothing in particular for a while, if you can.

4 FRIDAY
Moon Age Day 6   Moon Sign Sagittarius

Pleasurable pursuits may be more exciting than you expected and that could lead, in turn, to a more interesting day. If you can manage to get a break of some sort, today would be ideal. A very creative Libran is beginning to emerge, so perhaps you will take up some artistic hobbies, or become determined to make changes at home.

5 SATURDAY   *Moon Age Day 7   Moon Sign Capricorn*

Unfinished tasks need sorting out today, before you clear the decks for a new form of action that is waiting in the wings. Putting the finishing touches to anything is hard for Libra now because you have your sights on the next hurdle. However, at this point in time, you are going to discover that it is essential.

6 SUNDAY   *Moon Age Day 8   Moon Sign Capricorn*

This may be a day to go travelling and you would certainly enjoy the thrill of any chase that has a social aspect to it. Romance should also be highlighted, though these trends turn inwards towards those individuals you already know and perhaps towards an old flame that is starting to burn brightly again.

7 MONDAY   *Moon Age Day 9   Moon Sign Capricorn*

At work, you should discover that life is coming up trumps for you. The last week, or even two, might have been somewhat confusing, with concerns regarding home predominating. Now you are slightly more assertive in the wider world and anxious that people should know how capable you can be.

8 TUESDAY   *Moon Age Day 10   Moon Sign Aquarius*

Your main area of fulfilment today brings you back, once again, towards home and family. You face the challenges of life well but only by seeking the help and advice of those you love. You can see your way forward marked clearly, but can you make the wholesale changes that you instinctively know to be necessary?

9 WEDNESDAY   *Moon Age Day 11   Moon Sign Aquarius*

The communicative aspects of work serve you well now and bring you a good deal of joy. Mixing and mingling, even with people you haven't liked before, now becomes possible. It is less likely that you are making excuses for others and you may get to know what makes one or two mysterious individuals tick.

10 THURSDAY   *Moon Age Day 12   Moon Sign Pisces*

Work plays a much more important part in your life at this stage of the month than has been the case earlier. Now you have the chance to shine more and to show superiors what you are capable of. At the same time, your concern for home and family is not in the least diminished.

11 FRIDAY   *Moon Age Day 13   Moon Sign Pisces*

You will need to be as free from restrictions as you can manage today. There are people around who definitely seem to hold you back and who can prevent you from making the progress you would wish. In the seesaw kind of environment you inhabit just at present it is important to be on the ball.

12 SATURDAY   *Moon Age Day 14   Moon Sign Pisces*

Whilst it is clear that you enjoy communicating and getting your message across, this may now be slightly more difficult than it has been during the last couple of weeks. You are simply not able to get on-side with certain people, no matter how hard you try. It might be better to concentrate instead on issues and people you can change.

13 SUNDAY   *Moon Age Day 15   Moon Sign Aries*

Keep a low profile and make sure that your demands are realistic. The lunar low prevents you from following through with big plans for the next couple of days and so, for the short-term, aim to keep your expectations of life and of people moderate. Friendships should work out well around now.

14 MONDAY   *Moon Age Day 16   Moon Sign Aries*

You could be forgiven for believing that little is working out exactly as you may have wished. Although the day is not exactly gloomy, neither are you likely to find the sort of joy within it that you would wish. Keep an open mind concerning the needs and wants of family members, who come first in your thinking at this time.

137

15 TUESDAY
Moon Age Day 17   Moon Sign Taurus

You can expect some progress in your love life today, but as far as friendships are concerned you may need to keep an open mind about someone's behaviour, which might be giving cause for concern. Someone you haven't seen for a long time could make a reappearance in your life. Trends also favour all associations with the countryside and short journeys.

16 WEDNESDAY
Moon Age Day 18   Moon Sign Taurus

Enjoying personal liberty should seem to be somehow much easier today. Freedom of expression is paramount and you will think it necessary to let everyone know exactly how you feel. Fortunately you also have astrological trends around at the moment that point to diplomacy and tact.

17 THURSDAY
Moon Age Day 19   Moon Sign Taurus

Try to focus on minor obligations but don't get carried away with them. All in all, it's the bigger picture that counts and so you will be casting at least part of your mind far into the future. It is important that you get some time to yourself today, in order to do things that please only you.

18 FRIDAY
Moon Age Day 20   Moon Sign Gemini

Affairs of the heart have a great deal going for them this week and the romantic qualities of your nature are almost certain to show around now. This process is a two-way street, so you should not be in the least surprised to find that you are number one on someone else's list.

19 SATURDAY
Moon Age Day 21   Moon Sign Gemini

This is a period during which you will want to capitalise on the ability to do something new or different. Variety is the spice of life to Libra now and you may feel absolutely refreshed and vitalised, no matter how tired you feel, when you start to do something that is different from the norm.

20 SUNDAY
Moon Age Day 22   Moon Sign Cancer

Although it is hard work today to get your message across to others, both professionally and socially, it will be worth the extra effort. Librans who work on Sunday should have a better than average day and you should find that the sort of support you need is forthcoming during most of the day.

21 MONDAY
Moon Age Day 23   Moon Sign Cancer

Relationships should be on the up, even if you don't always have the time to explore them during the first half of today. Life finds ways of keeping you busy and it is likely that you will be skipping from one task to the next. All in all, you ought to find this a generally happy and productive day.

22 TUESDAY
Moon Age Day 24   Moon Sign Leo

The atmosphere at home should prove to be rewarding, which is part of the reason why you are spending less time on practical and professional matters right now. Try to relax and enjoy whatever today has to offer. Although the year is growing older, you can still revel in outdoor activities.

23 WEDNESDAY
Moon Age Day 25   Moon Sign Leo

There are advantageous situations today, particularly if you are a working Libran. Don't be put off by the sort of people who always seem to find problems in any situation and be sure that you put all your effort into new plans and schemes. The way friends are behaving could be something of a puzzle.

24 THURSDAY
Moon Age Day 26   Moon Sign Virgo

Romance and social matters have the ability to keep you smiling right now and you should find this to be a happy-go-lucky sort of day – just the kind that is meat and drink to your present mood. In the mix you should be able to find the time to tell someone close to you just how important they are. An interesting result could follow.

25 FRIDAY
Moon Age Day 27   Moon Sign Virgo

There is a new focus developing in your life and it comes along that much easier if you have taken things fairly steadily across the last couple of days. The quieter period will have allowed your mind to tick over steadily, sorting out a wealth of new plans that now make themselves truly apparent.

26 SATURDAY
Moon Age Day 28   Moon Sign Libra

Close to the end of October, the lunar high coincides with the weekend. The immediate result is one of greater excitement, plus a chance to follow your own will to a greater extent. Your powers of communication are now at their strongest and it isn't at all hard for you to impress a number of people.

27 SUNDAY
Moon Age Day 0   Moon Sign Libra

Today shows that your general level of good luck is increased and that social and romantic urges are much enhanced. This is a time when you are unlikely to allow anything to hold you back and during which you move forward progressively towards some longed-for objectives and opportunities.

28 MONDAY
Moon Age Day 1   Moon Sign Scorpio

Today will probably find you bringing some issue or other to a satisfactory conclusion. Whether you are involved in negotiations or practical jobs, the fact that your mind is ordered and your thinking sharp and focused is sure to help. Stay away from people you see as being essentially negative in attitude.

29 TUESDAY
Moon Age Day 2   Moon Sign Scorpio

Don't be afraid to make instant decisions in current endeavours and be sure to let those around you know what you are doing. This constant communication is very important indeed at present and ensures that everyone is pulling in the same direction. Some rules and regulations could seem entirely pointless.

30 WEDNESDAY   *Moon Age Day 3   Moon Sign Sagittarius*

You would be far happier today if you can follow independent pursuits and if you are not tied down to routines that others are setting for you. There are times when Librans can feel very fettered by convention and the social necessities of today can amplify this tendency.

31 THURSDAY   *Moon Age Day 4   Moon Sign Sagittarius*

There are practical setbacks today and these can lead to long delays when it comes to doing things you have planned. All you can do is to show a high degree of patience because shouting or stamping your feet simply won't help. In your friendships with others, you show yourself to be very loyal.

November 2019

1 FRIDAY
☿ *Moon Age Day 5   Moon Sign Sagittarius*

Your romantic encounters have a fulfilling quality about them now, making you keen to bring your emotions to the forefront and to enjoy what they mean for you and your partner. Although the year is now old, and the cold weather probably well underway, this would be an ideal day to make a trip designed purely for pleasure, rather than for business.

2 SATURDAY
☿ *Moon Age Day 6   Moon Sign Capricorn*

In the romantic area of life, it is clear at present that you want to take the leading role. Whilst this is not unusual for your zodiac sign, the situation is emphasised now to an even greater extent than usual. This is fine, just as long as the object of your desires is happy to have the situation this way.

3 SUNDAY
☿ *Moon Age Day 7   Moon Sign Capricorn*

Your mind is typically sharp today, offering a potentially satisfying and successful sort of Sunday. You will want to be mixing socially, and with all manner of people. Be careful. You cannot bring everyone round to your point of view and adding more layers of apparent evidence to your case probably won't help much.

4 MONDAY
☿ *Moon Age Day 8   Moon Sign Aquarius*

You won't allow yourself to be quite so waylaid by domestic matters today as might have been the case during the last week or so. The main reason for is that there is too much to be done in a practical sense. With little time to spare for niceties, you will need to be particularly careful not to offer inadvertent offence.

5 TUESDAY ☿ *Moon Age Day 9 Moon Sign Aquarius*

It is quite probable that you decide to please yourself today, no matter what anyone else thinks about the situation. It is very unusual for Libra to appear stubborn or bloody-minded, but it does happen now and again. Rather than offer offence as a result, it might be better to simply spend some time alone.

6 WEDNESDAY ☿ *Moon Age Day 10 Moon Sign Pisces*

In social affairs, you now enjoy a return to peak performance. The underlying, long-term trends now prevail and Libra shows itself in true colours. What you get from mixing with others is far greater than a simple chat. There is advice inherent in what people are saying that is well worth a second consideration.

7 THURSDAY ☿ *Moon Age Day 11 Moon Sign Pisces*

Your work life could prove to be an area of potential pressure, which is why you will do almost anything to let your hair down when the professional responsibilities are out of the way. You are very good right now at changing hats, which ought to provide for a very happy evening, and a release from tension on your part.

8 FRIDAY ☿ *Moon Age Day 12 Moon Sign Pisces*

Be liberal in your expectations of fun today, because that commodity comes in all shapes and sizes. If you avoid any particular advance conclusions, you take both joy and humour from what is happening around you. This is a time that works far better if you remain as spontaneous as Libra can be.

9 SATURDAY ☿ *Moon Age Day 13 Moon Sign Aries*

The quiet time of the month, brought about by the Moon in your opposite zodiac sign, begins today. The only difference this time around is that it probably will not be particularly quiet at all. Drawn into situations that are not of your choosing, you will be extremely voluble if forced down paths that do not appeal.

143

10 SUNDAY   ☿   *Moon Age Day 14*   *Moon Sign Aries*

Look out for repeated delays and setbacks, at least some of which cannot be avoided, no matter how hard you try. In fact, it isn't really worth trying at all. To do so represents the equivalent of trying to push water up a hill. Accept what life is offering with a smile and simply wait for more advantageous times.

11 MONDAY   ☿   *Moon Age Day 15*   *Moon Sign Taurus*

It seems likely that you are taking on some fairly heavy obligations but for today at least you should be viewing them in a sanguine way. Calm and clear, your mind can travel almost anywhere and it is obvious that the decisions you take are measured. That is why others trust you so much at present.

12 TUESDAY   ☿   *Moon Age Day 16*   *Moon Sign Taurus*

The spirit of harmony is around in terms of relationships. Although things will slow down somewhat, probably very sensibly, in the main progress is still likely and you have plenty of chances to make an impression. What matters most are the things you are saying to others and their responses.

13 WEDNESDAY ☿   *Moon Age Day 17*   *Moon Sign Taurus*

There could be a sense now that you have a clearer path towards a few of your dreams than has been the case for a while. Just remember, though, that some of them are just that – dreams. A dose of realism is called for, but not to the extent that you throw the baby out with the bath water. You must have horizons!

14 THURSDAY   ☿   *Moon Age Day 18*   *Moon Sign Gemini*

Any plans to make money at the moment will probably have to be left on hold. Your instinct for such matters is not strong right now and in any case less practical matters seem to be at the forefront of your mind. It would be sensible to seek the sound advice of an older relative or friend at some stage.

15 FRIDAY ☿ *Moon Age Day 19   Moon Sign Gemini*

In a social sense you can expect a generally fulfilling period and one during which there are plenty of opportunities to shine. Although there are things to be done that don't look especially satisfying or interesting, if you mix them in with more the more exciting aspects of life you should be able to turn this into an interesting day.

16 SATURDAY ☿ *Moon Age Day 20   Moon Sign Cancer*

In terms of your ability to join in with others, you should prove successful this Saturday. It may just be occurring to you how close Christmas is and so it isn't out of the question that you will embark on a shopping expedition. However, this is by no means certain because there are other things to do as well.

17 SUNDAY ☿ *Moon Age Day 21   Moon Sign Cancer*

Personal relationships should prove to be quite warm this Sunday and might mark the main focus as far as you are concerned. Libra is likely to be feeling quite romantic at present and won't be tardy when it comes to demonstrating the fact. Stay away from negative influences in terms of friends who are presently very pessimistic.

18 MONDAY ☿ *Moon Age Day 22   Moon Sign Leo*

Influential figures seem to be looking upon you very kindly at this time, offering new opportunities and probably brightening things up no end at work. Now is a time during which you could be looking for a new job or else thinking in terms of taking on different responsibilities.

19 TUESDAY ☿ *Moon Age Day 23   Moon Sign Leo*

A spirit of equality predominates today, which makes it easy for you to associate with just about anyone. Even in company that has seemed awkward before you now begin to shine noticeably. You don't look up to others or down on them. This is a sure sign of the egalitarian qualities of Libra.

20 WEDNESDAY ☿   *Moon Age Day 24*   *Moon Sign Leo*

The atmosphere in social settings is very good and a generally lively Libran is clearly on display at present. Although those around you might prove to be rather cautious in their approach to life, this cannot be said to be true of you. Reconciling your own needs with those of family members might prove difficult at times.

21 THURSDAY   *Moon Age Day 25*   *Moon Sign Virgo*

You might decide that some time spent on your own today is not wasted. The two days ahead of the lunar high are often quieter and more contemplative and this is very likely to be the case for you now. These moments offer you the chance to look at matters in a different light and to do some planning.

22 FRIDAY   *Moon Age Day 26*   *Moon Sign Virgo*

Although you can find no justifiable reason for things turning out awkwardly in a general sense, that is what is likely to happen. What matters most right now is the degree of patience that you bring to bear on matters. Tomorrow brings the lunar high and until then you may have to simply grit your teeth.

23 SATURDAY   *Moon Age Day 27*   *Moon Sign Libra*

Today looks like being a real success for Libra. With a host of supporting planetary aspects, as well as the lunar high, you are on form and ready for anything that life throws at you. Your confidence should be high and it appears that you have something akin to the Midas touch in terms of money.

24 SUNDAY   *Moon Age Day 28*   *Moon Sign Libra*

Most everyday issues begin to go according to plan and you are excellent today at cutting through red tape and getting to the heart of any issue. You can turn situations to your advantage and should not worry too much about details. It is the overall view of life that matters whilst the lunar high is around.

25 MONDAY   *Moon Age Day 29   Moon Sign Scorpio*

Life is likely to be generally fulfilling at this time and there are few people around who actively want to throw a spanner in the works. Nevertheless, you will have to watch out for accident-prone relatives or friends, some of whom are capable of creating a few problems for you.

26 TUESDAY   *Moon Age Day 0   Moon Sign Scorpio*

Life and love go hand in hand at this stage of the week. This is an interlude during which you won't have to work too hard in order to prove to those you love how important they are to you. There is a great deal of affection coming back in the other direction and a significant amount of happiness is the mutual result.

27 WEDNESDAY   *Moon Age Day 1   Moon Sign Sagittarius*

Personal setbacks are possible and you should take life as steadily as you can. Don't get involved in too many new ventures and show yourself willing to listen to the sound advice that is coming in. There is great support around at the moment if you go out and look for it.

28 THURSDAY   *Moon Age Day 2   Moon Sign Sagittarius*

Negotiations of almost any sort now work out well and there will be few more auspicious days than this for getting together with colleagues. Your view of life is sensible and you are also showing an unaccustomed humility that everyone respects. In social settings your way of talking helps.

29 FRIDAY   *Moon Age Day 3   Moon Sign Capricorn*

The planetary focus is now on relationships, both personal and more general. This is not a day on which you should expect to achieve a great deal in any concrete sense but that doesn't matter. The most important fact is that you are liked and respected. You can take great pleasure from this fact alone.

30 SATURDAY   *Moon Age Day 4   Moon Sign Capricorn*

In social matters you can prove to be a lively presence and almost anyone will be pleased to have you around. You can't get everything you want today in a material sense but it is clear that the things in life that are most important to you at present have little or nothing to do with money.

♎

December
2019

1 SUNDAY
Moon Age Day 5   Moon Sign Aquarius

You may prefer to stay at home today, which is a direct change of tack to what has been going on of late. Your creative potential looks good now, so perhaps you are already starting on the Christmas decorations or are addressing some other aspect of the upcoming festive season. Family attachments should feel secure.

2 MONDAY
Moon Age Day 6   Moon Sign Aquarius

Success in the workplace today is really a matter of how well you can get on with those you work alongside. You may be slightly impatient with some of your colleagues, particularly those who seem to deliberately misunderstand what you are trying to tell them. A little cultured patience can go a long way.

3 TUESDAY
Moon Age Day 7   Moon Sign Aquarius

This is a good time for leisure and pleasure activities of many different sorts. You are inclined to be rather energetic and may not want to spend too much time sitting around and thinking. Periods of high activity are not at all unusual for Libra but you will be busy at the moment, even by your own standards.

4 WEDNESDAY
Moon Age Day 8   Moon Sign Pisces

It looks as though you are going to be on top form at work today, which in turn could lead to a few successes you haven't really been expecting. If the social whirl has begun already, you need to be sure that you are getting enough rest. Perhaps try only going out six nights a week, leaving at least one on which you can rest!

5 THURSDAY
Moon Age Day 9   Moon Sign Pisces

Enjoying personal freedom is not at all difficult. It is time to capitalise on a new opportunity and to make the most of small financial gains that should be coming your way around now. If you don't do something novel or different at the moment, you might end up regretting it in the fullness of time.

6 FRIDAY
Moon Age Day 10   Moon Sign Aries

Your way of dealing with disputes that arise in your vicinity today could seem somehow inappropriate when seen from the perspective of others. If at all possible you should give people the benefit of the doubt, since there is a good chance you are being told the absolute truth as they see it.

7 SATURDAY
Moon Age Day 11   Moon Sign Aries

The lunar low can prove to be a disruptive influence today, possibly leading you to doubt your own abilities and certainly bringing a quieter Saturday than you have probably been expecting. What you can do now is to plan for Christmas, which is much closer than you might have realised.

8 SUNDAY
Moon Age Day 12   Moon Sign Aries

Putting things together on the material plane becomes less and less difficult. Few people are causing you too much concern and it is more than possible that a new relationship is about to commence. A high social profile on your part is the most satisfying way forward around now.

9 MONDAY
Moon Age Day 13   Moon Sign Taurus

Being one of the gang is the most enjoyable situation for you at present. Concern for those who are less well off than you is also important and putting yourself out on their behalf is no real hardship. You have plenty to keep you occupied, not least of all finishing off all those decorations and wrapping a host of presents.

10 TUESDAY   *Moon Age Day 14   Moon Sign Taurus*

A brief respite from some responsibilities allows you the time to get to grips with interests that are specifically yours. Don't be carried away by a material offer that looks far too good to be true. If you don't heed this advice, it is possible that you will learn in the fullness of time that someone is trying to deceive you.

11 WEDNESDAY   *Moon Age Day 15   Moon Sign Gemini*

Social contacts and loved ones can be in the market to offer you great favours today. In the countdown to the festive season you can do with all the support that is available and you should not be too worried about delegating some of the responsibility. As was the case yesterday, you need to be aware that confidence tricksters are about.

12 THURSDAY   *Moon Age Day 16   Moon Sign Gemini*

Dealings with those who are in a position of authority can be important today and you might need to be willing to cultivate their assistance and advice. When it comes to personal matters, no matter what other people tell you, it is important to make up your own mind about your own course of action in the end.

13 FRIDAY   *Moon Age Day 17   Moon Sign Cancer*

This is a marvellous period for twosomes and a time when you will be happiest in the arms of your lover. Present planetary trends make it possible for you to fully express yourself and there are likely to be some incredible compliments coming your way. Do an extra bit of work today in order to save time for fun later.

14 SATURDAY   *Moon Age Day 18   Moon Sign Cancer*

In terms of your career you should be shining now and the same is true if you are presently involved in any form of education. In any area of life, though, you should be quite well aware of the people who can do you the greatest favours right now and you would be rather foolish to turn away their kindness.

15 SUNDAY
Moon Age Day 19   Moon Sign Cancer

Close ties may not bring out the best in you today, and if you feel this is the case you would be better off spending time with casual friends. There is room to change your mind at work but less flexibility in home-based matters. People tend to be demanding around now so you could find that you will need to be in three places at once.

16 MONDAY
Moon Age Day 20   Moon Sign Leo

Support is available where finances are concerned, even if this is only in an advisory sense. Today could seem to bring a slight reversal in fortune but any disappointments are likely to be short in duration. Not everything can be expected to go quite as well as you would wish but you remain generally cheerful.

17 TUESDAY
Moon Age Day 21   Moon Sign Leo

This could turn out to be one of the best days of the month to be seen by others. As a result, it would be good at some stage to put on your best clothes and shine for all you are worth. In personal relationships, avoid the little green-eyed monster of jealousy; if you don't you could end up looking somewhat foolish.

18 WEDNESDAY
Moon Age Day 22   Moon Sign Virgo

In a financial sense, this is a time of short-term increase, so you may as well enjoy the gains while they last. Not that cash is likely to stay with you long at this time of year. You may get the chance to get ahead in something that is quite important to you and won't be tardy when it comes to having your say.

19 THURSDAY
Moon Age Day 23   Moon Sign Virgo

Everyday life should run fairly smoothly now and there will be plenty of time for enjoyment, which is what is needed at this time of year. If the approach of Christmas becomes a bore, then most of the happiness surrounding it disappears altogether. This shouldn't bother you, though, as you are probably as excited as a child.

20 FRIDAY
Moon Age Day 24   Moon Sign Libra

Today finds you fully ensconced in the lunar high, with none of the attendant difficulties that took the shine off yesterday. Enjoy the positive trends, both socially and with regard to romance. A great deal of energy goes into making today special, and things stay that way throughout the upcoming period.

21 SATURDAY
Moon Age Day 25   Moon Sign Libra

Plans that are presently on the boil get an extra boost and there is no stopping you on your personal quest to make the sort of splash that is bound to get you noticed. There are quite a few people around at this time whose sole desire in life seems to be to support you. Take opportunities as and when they arise.

22 SUNDAY
Moon Age Day 26   Moon Sign Scorpio

You might feel that your partner, or maybe a family member, is being rather bossier than you are willing to accept. Remember the time of year and bite your tongue. When you finally get around to understanding what the irritation actually is, you should be glad that you managed to keep your cool.

23 MONDAY
Moon Age Day 27   Moon Sign Scorpio

Look around for some intelligent and interesting conversations today because you can gain a great deal from them. This is not really a day during which you would be happy to spend time alone. On the contrary, the more the merrier seems to be your adage at present.

24 TUESDAY
Moon Age Day 28   Moon Sign Sagittarius

There should be plenty of opportunity to talk to your life partner today and to do so could find you reaching a newer and better understanding of matters in a general sense. Not everyone out there in the wider world is going to be in tune with your ideas but that shouldn't bother you too much at present.

153

25 WEDNESDAY *Moon Age Day 29   Moon Sign Sagittarius*

This ought to be a particularly enjoyable Christmas Day in almost every respect. Don't be at all surprised if you have the urge to travel somewhere, perhaps to see relatives or friends. Although you can really enjoy having fun, it is just possible that you will feel restless, which is why you need to be on the move.

26 THURSDAY *Moon Age Day 0   Moon Sign Capricorn*

Relationships form the chief interest now so it is especially likely that you will be spending time with relatives, even given how common that is at this time of year. If the traditions of Christmas start to get on your nerves, accept that it's all part of family life and, ultimately, it all has its place in your sentimental mind.

27 FRIDAY *Moon Age Day 1   Moon Sign Capricorn*

A quite independent stance means that you are seeking freedom from emotional demands today. What you want now is simply to have fun. The more you spread the social net, the greater is the likelihood that this will be the case. New friends could be coming into your life now.

28 SATURDAY *Moon Age Day 2   Moon Sign Capricorn*

This looks like being an extremely good time for problem solving. Perhaps take a day out from the usual holiday activities and instead put your mind to the test. This is always a good exercise for you, though you should not make more out of your findings than they really mean. You certainly shouldn't struggle with a lack of confidence now.

29 SUNDAY *Moon Age Day 3   Moon Sign Aquarius*

For some reason you are listening less to what others have to say today, and this fact might prove to be to your detriment. Watch out for a tendency to overlook details and, whilst you are looking at a broad overview of life make sure that you deal with specifics too.

30 MONDAY   *Moon Age Day 4   Moon Sign Aquarius*

It is the domestic arena that offers the best chance of interest and happiness today. Although you can still be making gains if you are at work, the actions or ideas of colleagues could be taking the shine off certain, otherwise excellent, situations. When work is out of the way you should find yourself better able to relax.

31 TUESDAY   *Moon Age Day 5   Moon Sign Pisces*

Despite a few petty problems in personal relationships which you can deal with early in the day, you can turn your focus solely towards having a good time on this New Year's Eve. Give all you've got to the celebrations and don't take yourself, or anyone else, too seriously.

RISING SIGNS FOR LIBRA

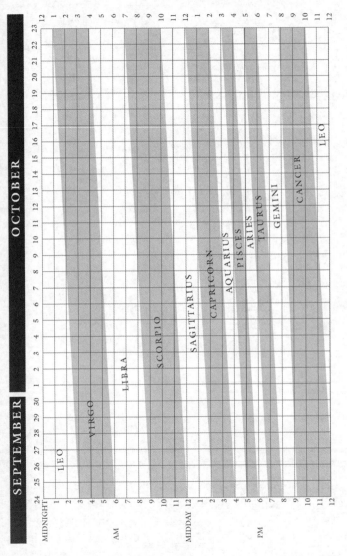

THE ZODIAC, PLANETS AND CORRESPONDENCES

The Earth revolves around the Sun once every calendar year, so when viewed from Earth the Sun appears in a different part of the sky as the year progresses. In astrology, these parts of the sky are divided into the signs of the zodiac and this means that the signs are organised in a circle. The circle begins with Aries and ends with Pisces.

Taking the zodiac sign as a starting point, astrologers then work with all the positions of planets, stars and many other factors to calculate horoscopes and birth charts and tell us what the stars have in store for us.

The table below shows the planets and Elements for each of the signs of the zodiac. Each sign belongs to one of the four Elements: Fire, Air, Earth or Water. Fire signs are creative and enthusiastic; Air signs are mentally active and thoughtful; Earth signs are constructive and practical; Water signs are emotional and have strong feelings.

It also shows the metals and gemstones associated with, or corresponding with, each sign. The correspondence is made when a metal or stone possesses properties that are held in common with a particular sign of the zodiac.

Finally, the table shows the opposite of each star sign – this is the opposite sign in the astrological circle.

Placed	Sign	Symbol	Element	Planet	Metal	Stone	Opposite
1	Aries	Ram	Fire	Mars	Iron	Bloodstone	Libra
2	Taurus	Bull	Earth	Venus	Copper	Sapphire	Scorpio
3	Gemini	Twins	Air	Mercury	Mercury	Tiger's Eye	Sagittarius
4	Cancer	Crab	Water	Moon	Silver	Pearl	Capricorn
5	Leo	Lion	Fire	Sun	Gold	Ruby	Aquarius
6	Virgo	Maiden	Earth	Mercury	Mercury	Sardonyx	Pisces
7	Libra	Scales	Air	Venus	Copper	Sapphire	Aries
8	Scorpio	Scorpion	Water	Pluto	Plutonium	Jasper	Taurus
9	Sagittarius	Archer	Fire	Jupiter	Tin	Topaz	Gemini
10	Capricorn	Goat	Earth	Saturn	Lead	Black Onyx	Cancer
11	Aquarius	Waterbearer	Air	Uranus	Uranium	Amethyst	Leo
12	Pisces	Fishes	Water	Neptune	Tin	Moonstone	Virgo